W9-BAA-752

KITCHEN TABLE
BIRD BOOK

WRITTEN BY
JOHN HAM

ILLUSTRATED BY
DAVID MOHRHARDT

TwoPeninsula Press
Lansing, Michigan
March 1984
Fifth Printing, 1990

Table Of Contents

About This Book

The birds depicted in this book are arranged according to size, moving from the smallest birds in the front of the book to the largest at the back. Size here is determined by body length alone, and you'll see that measurement, in inches, printed in the upper right corner on each of the plates. We believe this to provide the simplest means of finding in this book any unknown bird that appears before you. Simply guess the bird's body length, then turn to that portion of the book showing birds of about that length. Once there, flipping pages back and forth in those approximate lengths should locate the bird for you readily. If you know the name of the bird, you can use the alphabetized index to species printed inside the back cover to locate the plate and information.

This *Kitchen Table Bird Book* grew to publication over a period of three years, and changed form in that time gradually to fit what has seemed its most practical purpose—use by residents of our Great Lakes region who spend most of their bird-watching time at home, inside, looking out windows at feeding, bathing birds. The 77 species discussed and portrayed here represent the most common small birds that come to feeders, or which might land on marsh edge or lawn or woodlands of the type often seen from kitchen windows of this region. The companion *Coat Pocket Bird Book* contains another 80 species, most of which will be seen afield, but some of which may also come to your feeder. The placement of some species in one or the other of these books was in some cases arbitrarily decided, though our intention all along has been to provide one book for home use, one for field use.

These two books were designed primarily for the casual, beginning, and intermediate birdwatcher, though we have been pleased by the positive reception given to the books by birding veterans with hundreds of species included on their "life lists." In fact, we believe any birdwatcher, of whatever experience, will find these books valuable and useful reference works. Together, the two books do not include all the birds that visit, nest, or live year-round in this region, but the 157 species collectively represent, we estimate, 90-plus percent of all the millions of birds that will be seen here. Consequently, if you eventually do see all the species depicted in these books, you will be a birdwatching professional.

Other Bird Guides

One or the other, or both, of two important bird guides would be useful to have nearby when using our two books. They are Peterson's *Field Guide to Birds East of the Rockies,* and Robbin's *Birds of North America.* Both are commonly available in bookstores and at some of the larger newsstands. We also sell them to readers through our *Michigan Book Central* division, Box 30034, Lansing 48909. Both are excellent references for *identifying* any and all birds of our region. Identification is their purpose and they do it well. However, they do include hundreds of birds most of us will never see, and the information they provide on each species is quite limited, simply because there isn't room for more. By contrast, our books include fewer birds, but tell you more about each; and the birds included are those you stand the strongest chance of seeing here.

Suggestions From Readers

Here are a few random suggestions on backyard birding which readers have suggested and which we have found useful. We feel they will help you enjoy this growing, interesting study of bird life, and we pass them on to you here with that purpose in mind:

1. To triple the number of your feathered visitors, double the number of feeders you place out. It's almost a mathematical certainty that this will happen, though no one seems able to explain why. Make one a window feeder and one a platform feeder, or hang one from a tree limb or porch eave and then scatter seeds over a 6 to 10 foot circle on open ground, on snow, on your lawn, on an adjacent flat roof, or wherever you can watch the feathered follies. To further increase bird visitation, make fresh water available.

2. If birds injure or kill themselves flying into your windows, try placing an open platform type feeder within a couple of feet of your largest window area. We've found that birds which fly off such a feeder frequently bang into the window, but seldom injure themselves; apparently they can't get up enough speed in a short distance to cause themselves much more than a headache. For other protections against bird/window collisions, see "About Birdfeeding and Birdfeeders" on pages 150-151 in this book.

3. If a bird does knock itself silly against your window, take it into a warm room and keep it in a closed box for as long as an hour or two. We once revived a bird an hour after it collided with our window, then placed in on a tree limb where it sat without moving for another full two hours before flying away.

4. If marauding cats and dogs are a neighborhood problem, save your sanity and preserve local peace by *outwitting* the four-foots. Place obstacles in their secret paths that will force them into the open where birds can see them. A wide strip of sheet metal wrapped around a tree five or six feet above ground will prevent cats from climbing that tree. Chicken wire fencing placed at the base of a bush will prevent cats from hiding where they can dash out for surprise attacks. hanging feeders over open areas, or placing seeds on the ground in locations where birds can see all around for several feet will help protect the feathered ones. Birds can escape most attacks and can frustrate cats eternally if given a bit of help. Also, if you make friends with local cats, you may be able to catch the cat and save a bird it's just caught. Many times, we've pried open local cat jaws, released birds, and then seen the birds fly away, apparently uninjured. But you need to be on good terms with the cat in order to catch it in those critical few moments just after a bird is caught.

5. Attach a stick or length of dried tree limb to a platform feeder so birds can land on a familiar perch before hopping to the feeder itself.

6. Some veteran birdwatchers urge their friends to avoid bags of mixed seeds offered in many grocery stores and supermarkets. They say these convenient looking mixtures frequently include seeds which birds shun, and that they also include many low value seeds. The best way to buy seeds is in bulk at grain elevators, through local Audubon Society chapters, and at hardware stores. Concentrate on striped and black sunflower seeds, white millet, cracked corn, and niger (also called thistle) seed.

Plumage Changes

Throughout this book, Dave Mohrhardt's paintings mainly depict birds in their spring plumage. Birds molt in late summer and early fall, and many look quite different at that time. Some remain in altered plumage through the winter, the American Goldfinch being a prime example of this. The males are a bright chrome yellow during the spring and summer breeding months, but dull down to a soft mouse gray during the winter and retain only a hint of yellow at that time. The females are less colorful in spring and summer, but they also soften to a dull gray in the fall. If you are aware of these molt changes in those seasons, you can use habits, habitat, size, and food preferences as alternate means of determining the identity of birds that puzzle you, or which don't seem to be included in this book.

Keeping Notes Is Important

We have left ample margins and plenty of white space on the plates and we urge you to write into this book your observations about the birds you see. Also, there are two checklists in the back of the book, one to record basic information on birds depicted in this book, and a second, comprehensive list of all birds recorded here from earliest times. The white space and checklists are included here to increase the value of this book and provide a meaningful extension of your birdwatching activities.

Some Who Helped

No book has ever been published that did not require the efforts of many people, and the most useful and interesting books draw on the wisdom and information of a lot of people. So it has been with this book. We haven't space to name everyone involved, but a few were primary: Jim Purvis of Lansing worked diligently to weed out technical problems during an advanced stage of manuscript review. Kathryn Breighner of Petoskey and Martha McKee of Milwaukee reviewed the essays from their respective geographical perspectives and made valuable suggestions on northern Michigan and Wisconsin bird-watching activities in those regions. John Felsing of Lansing, a superb bird artist in his own right, kept us out of confusion when it loomed during final preparation of plates and essays. Gijsbert van Frankenhuyzen of Bath and Leianne Wright of Lansing contributed heavily to the final design and typography. Kris Krumanaker and Ruth Jones were patient and helpful during final typographical preparation and review and their knowledge in this area was crucial to completion of the book. But we are well aware that John Ham and Dave Mohrhardt were here first, and did most of the work, and that this is definitely their book. All the rest of us were simply helpers along the way.

Russell McKee
Lansing, January 1984

The Architecture Of A Bird

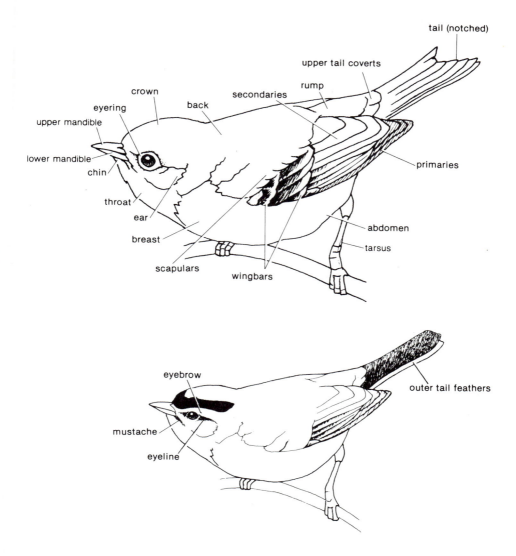

Note: The presence of an eyering and wingbars are two common things to look for when identifying many songbirds. In the illustrations above, you'll note these characteristics are present in the first bird, but are absent in the other.

Ruby-throated Hummingbird

Archilochus colubris

Bird watchers are always thrilled at the sight of a hummingbird appearing like a large colorful insect at local Great Lakes feeders. The green back of this tiny bundle of energy is plain to see, but the flaming red throat is seen only when light strikes the feathers just right. Otherwise, the throat looks black. Our observations differ from the paintings shown in other bird guides, which depict the red throat as quite obvious. It is not. The main point to remember is that we have only one species of hummingbird in the Great Lakes region, so if you see what appears to be a large green insect with a long bill and wings that move so fast they blur, it's a Rubythroat. Special feeders filled with colored sugar-water will attract them, and certain flowers invite the tiny creatures. It is not true that flowers must be red to be visited by a hummer, though it helps.

The flight of the hummingbird is a sight worth seeing; hovering in place over a blossom is easy. So is backward flight, and the dash from flower to flower is rapid. Most of the time you will see just one hummer at a flower or feeder, as Hummingbirds are not very sociable. Mating is also a fleeting occurrence and pairs do not shop together for nectar. The females attend to family chores after mating, while the males go off to drink nectar.

Mother hummingbirds build a unique nest, which is formed into a little cup about one inch in diameter and one inch deep. She uses bud scales, plant down, and fine fibers to fashion the nest and the neat structure is attached to a horizontal tree limb. It may be 50 feet above ground, and may be placed in any of various species of trees. It's generally in a shady spot, however, and here she lays two pure white eggs the size of a Spanish peanut. She incubates them for two weeks, and then feeds the fly-sized young a diet of nectar and tiny insects. For two and a half weeks the hatchlings remain in the nest. Some male youngsters develop red on the throat before they leave the nest, though this coloration typically appears a bit later.

Food for these diminutive birds includes nectar and the various tiny insects which inhabit blossoms that contain such sweet juice. Gladioli, nasturtiums, and cannas are some of the flowers that attract hummers. Tubular feeders, filled with a 4 to 1 ratio of colored water and sugar, will often provide you with the delightful experience of watching a hummingbird in flight. Rarely will you see one perched, as they are dynamos of motion. Rubythroats are the only hummingbirds seen in the eastern U.S., though Rufous Hummingbirds have been reported on one or two unverified occasions in southwestern Michigan. Rubythroats go south in the fall and remain in southern Florida and Texas, and in Central and South America, until longer days and warmer temperatures draw them back to us once again in spring.

Key Natural History References: Bent 1940, Pitelka 1942, Pickens 1936.

Female

Male

Ruby-crowned Kinglet *Regulus calendula*
Golden-crowned Kinglet *Regulus satrapa*

These tiny birds are hard to follow as they scramble about in a thicket. Both are olive-gray birds smaller than most warblers. The male Ruby-crowned Kinglet has a scarlet crown patch, usually concealed, but erect when he is excited. Both male and female Rubycrowns have clearly-defined white and black wing bars and conspicuous white broken eye-rings. Golden-crowned Kinglets have a whitish eyebrow stripe. Both male and female Goldencrowns have a bright crown patch—yellow in the female, orange in the male, bordered by black.

The Ruby-crowned Kinglet's song is three or four high notes, quite loud, and a chant: *tee tee tee, tew tew tew tew, ti-dadee, ti-dadee, ti-dadee.* The Goldencrown male sings in a series of high thin notes that ascend then drop away into chattering.

Usually we see Rubycrowns only briefly during spring and fall migrations as they pass through the Great Lakes region on their way to nest in Canada or winter in our southern states. However, the Goldencrown has been extending its range in recent years and now is found throughout the Great Lakes region in the winter and to a lesser extent farther north in the summer. However, numbers of these birds are not large in many locales, so if you see them it will prove a special treat.

Nests of both kinglets are deep cups placed in spruce or pine trees below the level of the horizontal supporting twigs. Some nests are four inches deep, so the tiny birds are completely hidden when sitting on the eggs. Moss, lichens, fur, and feathers are used to build the nest and are often woven together with hair. Eggs average eight or nine in number and are whitish with brown spots. The female sits on the eggs for about 12 days, and when the young hatch, the males join in the task of feeding and protecting the family. Parents search the bark of trees for the minute insects that their young eat; occasionally you will see kinglets hovering or fluttering in flight as they look for food. Some insects are captured in flight, though gleaning insects from trees is the more common habit.

Kinglets may pass through as a wave during migration. In winter they may be seen with Chickadees and Creepers, usually in pine or spruce woods, fluttering quickly in their restless search for food. These diminutive creatures are a delight to watch—if you can follow them.

Key Natural History References, both birds: Andrle 1971, Bent 1948, Forbush 1929, Lepthien and Bock 1976.

Golden-crowned Kinglet (top)   3½-4 inches
Ruby-crowned Kinglet (bottom)   4 inches

Male

Female

Male

Female

Blue-gray Gnatcatcher *Polioptila caerulea*

Blue-gray gnatcatchers are much smaller than sparrows, and they move about so nervously that it's sometimes hard to follow them with binoculars. Usually you see these birds high in a tree; they have a blue-gray back, white breast, plain eye-ring, and a relatively long tail bordered with white feathers. The habit of flicking that long tail, and their constant movement on tree branches, will help you locate and identify them.

The nest of the gnatcatcher is an eye-catching sight. The structure is built on a fork of branches in a deciduous tree forming a tiny cup that resembles a knot on the underside of a horizontal limb. The nest is made of plant down, lichens, and fine plant fibers that are bound together with string or silk from cocoons or spider webs. Frequently the diameter of the open top is less than the diameter at the bottom of the little cup. Both birds build the structure, starting a week or two before the eggs are laid; the nest is similar to that of the neat, compact structure made by the hummingbird. If, before the nest is completed, something happens to make the nest site undesirable (some other birds building their nest too close by, for example), it is this bird's peculiar habit to move away, find a second site for its nest, but return time after time to transport materials of the partially or completely finished first nest to use in building the second.

Normally four or five bluish-white eggs with numerous brown spots are laid by the female. The birds take turns sitting on the clutch and are usually completely out of sight in the deep nest. Hatching occurs after 13 days of incubation; the young remain in the nest for about 11 days. Loads of tiny insects must be brought to the rapidly growing family. During this time the parents are so intensely preoccupied with feeding their young that they ignore humans nearby and will fly directly to the nest with food rather than taking a cautious, more secretive approach. Add to this the fact that their young become noisy soon after hatching and it makes finding the nest of this gnatcatcher somewhat easier.

This is a tiny bird, but keep in mind that you can determine what it is by the obvious white feathers on the edges of its tail, and by its jumpy behavior. It is a common sight in the Lower Peninsula during the summer, less common in the U.P. These diminutive creatures spend the winter along the southeastern coast of the U.S. from North Carolina to Texas. Some observers in Florida have reported large numbers of Blue-Gray Gnatcatchers in specific areas of the state in January and February. However, many of them apparently continue on farther south to winter in Mexico and Central America.

Key Natural History References: Forbush 1929, Root 1967 and 1970, Nice 1932.

Red-breasted Nuthatch *Sitta canadensis*
White-breasted Nuthatch *Sitta carolinensis*

Both these birds may visit your feeders at any time of year, as both are year-round residents of the Great Lakes region. However, the Red-breasted Nuthatch tends to nest mainly in the northern half of the Great Lakes region, as well as north into Canada, so it may not appear in the southern half of our region during the warm months.

We list these two together because of similarities of range and habit though there are distinctive differences as well that will help you tell them apart. The Whitebreast, for example, is 6 inches in body length, the Redbreast only about 4 inches. The Redbreast is more commonly seen in association with conifers, as the seeds of such trees are its food mainstay, while the Whitebreast favors deciduous trees and feeds more commonly on insects, which it gleans by hopping along and around tree trunks and down main tree limbs. But these are preferences, not absolute requirements, and both birds, for example, do consume tree-living insects as well as seeds, fruit, acorns, and feeding station suet. Both also seem determined to live upside down and almost always will approach suet and feeder seeds from above, hopping downward head first along a tree trunk, porch support, or feeder hanger to reach the food.

The voices of both these birds are distinctively nasal, the Whitebreast uttering a steady *yank, yank, yank* throughout the year as it moves along a tree trunk; the Redbreast uttering a more high-pitched *ank, ank, ank,* with a tinhorn quality.

Whitebreasts mate for life, and are not shy about coming to feeders; the Redbreasts are a bit less interested in civilization, and because the southern half of the Great Lakes region has fewer conifers, it also has fewer Redbreasts.

Whitebreasts nest in tree cavities from near ground level anywhere up to the tops of large trees. They favor rotted out knotholes, old woodpecker holes, and nest boxes. On occasion they will hollow out their own hole. Whatever hole they select, they will fill it first with coarse material such as twigs, and then inner-line it with feathers and bits of animal fur, soft stuff to cradle the 5 or 6 precious eggs the female lays. The eggs have a white base and are flecked with reddish brown.

Redbreasts follow much the same nesting practices, again using natural cavities or hollowing out their own nest hole to deposit, again, 5 or 6 eggs with roughly the same color markings. However, Redbreast eggs as you might imagine are a bit smaller than those of the larger Whitebreast.

Because these two birds are so similar in size, habit, and range, it's fortunate for the bird-watcher that they at least have a difference of chest color!

Key Natural History References, both birds: Bent 1948, Butts 1931, Forbush 1929, Kilhorn 1968, Lawrence 1952.

Red-breasted Nuthatch (top)   4½ inches
White-breasted Nuthatch (bottom)   5-6 inches

House Wren *Troglodytes aedon*

The chattering, rattling song of the brown House Wren forces the attention of any listener. Their vivacious behavior and jolly singing are features that lead many birders to love this little wren. Many observers have seen House Wrens invade the nests of other birds, and it's known that they will even puncture the eggs if they can sneak into a nest. Their consumption of insects is helpful to us but this disturbing habit reduces their overall value.

The House Wren is the plainest of the wrens and is smaller than a House Sparrow—about four and one-half inches long. This small, energetic bird is a gray-brown color with a very light eye-ring. You can distinguish the House Wren from the Marsh Wren because the House Wren has an unstreaked back, and it also lacks the dark belly of other wrens.

In April, the male House Wrens arrive in our latitude to establish territories and select several boxes or holes for a summer home. The little birds are notorious for nesting in very unusual places such as old shoes, flowerpots, and other small receptacles. The male gathers hundreds of twigs and starts several nests in anticipation of the arrival of the female. When she arrives, she selects a mate and a nest site. She may start her own nest, or she may throw out all his twigs and gather her own for a site he chose. Twigs may be piled four inches deep, after which a small depression is made for the eggs.

The eggs are attractive homes for the embryos. The basic color is white but that may be totally obscured by deep brown or purplish blotches. The energetic little bird lays six or seven eggs in one clutch—one that nested in our yard laid a batch of nine. The female will incubate them for about 13 days by herself, while the male floods the air with his song from a nearby perch. Once the young are hatched, the father helps his mate feed the brood and does his share of housecleaning chores. If the brood is the first one of the season, the mother may leave the family early to start another nest, often picking a new mate, and leaving her young in the care of their father.

Grasshoppers, beetles and caterpillars are delicacies the House Wrens collect as they scramble about in thickets and hedges. They like territories that are somewhat open, rather than dense woods. If nest boxes are placed in your yard, be sure each box is a bit isolated, because wrens do not like other birds too close to their active nests.

Wrens enjoy living near people and will bolster your spirits with their bubbling vitality and song. Most of them leave us in late fall to join the flights of House Wrens that travel to the Gulf states and south to Argentina for the winter. Look for them to return to states east of the Rockies and north of the Appalachians—including the Great Lakes states—each April.

Key Natural History References: Kendeigh 1916, Forbush 1929, Bent 1948, Odum and Johnston 1951.

Pine Siskin *Carduelis pinus*

If, because of the Pine Siskin's busy movements at your feeders, you can only see the backs of these birds, mixed in with a group of their friends the Common Redpolls, you might think of them all as the same species. From a slight distance they do look very much alike in size, color, and habit. But male Redpolls have red caps and females have black chins, while Pine Siskins have neither. Also, if you see some flashes of *yellow* on wings and tail, it's a Siskin, not a Redpoll. Even though the yellow on rump and wings is limited, it can be seen as they move about and fly. Some guidebooks show this yellow to be much more prominent than it is. My experience is that you can see it, but only when flashed during flight or movement. Finally, Pine Siskins have heavier streaking on their breasts and a less reddish tone overall.

These birds move about in noisy bunches, their call a wheezy trill, and they come to our feeders on a very irregular schedule. Some winters we don't see them at all. However, the tiny black thistle seed called niger is their most treasured feeder food, so we keep a supply out there all the time on the chance they might turn up. Siskins have short, sharp bills that can readily crack these tiny seeds from their shells.

Most Siskin nesting takes place in western Canada and the northern parts of our Great Lakes and northeastern states. They build their nests far out on the wobbly branches of conifers and often build rather close to other Siskin neighbors. If they were people, they would probably live in a city.

Also, for such small birds, they build rather large nests of rootlets, grass, feathers, and twigs. Eggs are four or five in number and have brown and black spots over a pale greenish-blue shell. Pappa feeds Mamma and defends a tiny territory while she incubates these little emeralds for 13 days, after which the young hatch and stay in the nest about 15 days. His searching for food may be in company with other males of his kind, all of which seems to add to the group spirit of Siskins. Included in the normal diet are seeds from hemlocks, alders, and cedars. These little birds also help control many pests that attack forests of evergreens. In fact, woe be to insects that gather on Siskin nesting trees; they're sure to be turned into Siskin dinners. As feeding is carried out in group situations nearly all the time, the reduction of such insects in certain areas may be substantial.

During the winter, Pine Siskins migrate south as far as Florida and Mexico, but many lag behind and appear at our feeders in cold weather. You can help them, and keep them close, when they do appear. Simply keep your feeders filled. Even if larger birds take over your feeders, they'll scatter seeds about sufficiently so you'll see flocks of Redpolls, Siskins, and Goldfinches searching every square inch of ground to secure a meal.

Key Natural History References: Bent 1968, Weaver and West 1943.

18

Pine Siskin   4½-5 inches

Black-and-white Warbler *Mniotilta varia*

These beautiful little creatures have a richly colored coat and will charm any birdwatcher with their songs and actions. Their habit of moving up and down a tree trunk with uncommon ease gives them the nickname of "creeper." This bird is a little shorter than a House Sparrow, about five inches long, and has a trim body build. White and black streaks run *lengthwise* over the whole back and head, and the breast is snow white. Tall deciduous trees are the delight of the Black-and-white Warbler, the type of tree that attracts insects and allows this bird to run up and down the trunk looking for food. The tree climbing activities of these birds are similar to those of the nuthatch.

Black-and-white Warblers arrive here in the Great Lakes region in April, and when I see this crisply colored bird, I know that more warblers of other types will soon be visiting; these are among the earliest.

Black-and-white Warblers nest throughout the Great Lakes region, with the males arriving first in the spring and becoming noticeably agitated when the females drop in a bit later. After courtship and mating, the female builds a bulky nest on the ground, on a stump, or at the base of a tree. Nesting materials include bark, grass, sticks, rootlets, and hair of any passing animal. One brood of four or five is hatched each season from the clutch of creamy white eggs that are spotted with a variegated brown. After only 11 days of incubation, the young hatch and soon fluff out with a coat of gray puffy feathers. In less than two weeks, they begin crawling about over the nearest tree trunks looking for food. By mid-summer, the young have feathered out completely and look little different from their parents. They then may be seen together, moving about over any tree trunk in the neighborhood of the nest site, digging at every crack and crevice for beetles, caterpillars, spiders, and ants. It is clear that in this way Black-and-white Warblers help in the control of many tree-destroying species of insects.

The Black-and-white Warbler seems set apart from other warblers because of its tree-climbing behavior; it alone among the warbler family seems comfortable scampering along tree trunks and up and down large tree branches. It spends a large part of its time on vertical or sharply angled surfaces, on which it moves quickly and easily, upside down or right side up. It is sure-footed and, unlike the woodpeckers, does not have to use its tail for support.

Black-and-whites winter in Florida, southern Texas, and the Gulf states, but many travel as far south as South America. Be sure to listen for their thin *weesee-weesee-weesee* trill each spring, however, when they return to our region for their nesting.

Key Natural History References: Forbush 1929, Griscom 1957, Harrison 1975.

Male

Female

Common Yellowthroat *Geothlypis trichas*

All across eastern North America this jumpy little bird can be seen—though not frequently—from April to October. Marshy areas nearly always have their quota of Yellowthroats, but these birds will also hop around in the low vegetation along roadsides, in meadows, and near lakes and streams. If you see the male, with his wide black mask bordered with white, you will easily remember him; the olive green back and yellow breast are also striking. The female and the young have no mask, so it's easy to confuse them with other warblers. This is one of those species you'll probably not see in your backyard, though you never can tell. Mostly you'll have to seek out these little creatures if you want a glimpse of them, since they prefer wild lands, especially those grown up with briars and low brush, and they seldom come near towns or suburbs.

The Yellowthroat's song is interpreted as *witchity-witchity-witchity-witch.* These birds are only four and one-half inches long and have short tails. You can expect to see them scrambling around on reeds, cattails, and willows that are near or in a marsh. If you hear their distinctive song, just wait for them to appear on the tops of some aquatic plants.

Nests are built anywhere from a few inches to three or four feet above the water or ground. The structural materials include weeds, leaves, grass, ferns, and hair; nests are often located along a small creek or in the midst of a marsh. They are always well concealed. Cowbirds love to add their eggs to the clutch of a Yellowthroat, and I have personally watched as a tiny pair of them attempted to feed a large gray Cowbird youngster.

A normal clutch of Yellowthroat eggs numbers four and they are white with gray and brown spots. Females warm the eggs for 12 days to hatch the young and the male sings loudly from a nearby perch while she is sitting. Both adults feed insects to the young and the gypsy moth is one of their favorite meals. The young at the time of hatching are nearly naked and their eyes are sealed shut. Within minutes of emerging from their eggs they get their first meal, usually an insect. On the fourth day their eyes open for the first time; on the eighth the feathers have grown to such an extent that the young have a smooth and pleasing appearance. On the ninth day they are ready to leave the nest and will do so at the least disturbance. The young leave the nest for good when they are about 10 days old.

Late in October the Yellowthroats move south across the U.S. in a wide front. In winter some of them reside in our southernmost states, but most move on to Central America as far south as Panama. Your best opportunity to see this bird is during the summer at some marshy region near your home.

Key Natural History References: Forbush 1929, Stewart 1953.

Female

Male

Nashville Warbler *Vermivora ruficapilla*

Nashville Warblers are tiny and jumpy. Their migratory flight follows the eastern coasts of Central America, Mexico, and along the Mississippi Valley. When they enter the United States they spread out, and nests have been found from Minnesota to New Jersey and New England. Probably the majority of the Nashvilles nest in parts of Canada just north of our border, but they may nest in the northern areas of the Great Lakes states as well.

Every year for the last ten years, this four and three-quarter inch bundle of energy has visited my birdbath in spring and fall. Look for a warbler that sports a gray head, yellow on the breast and under the chin, and a white eye-ring. This warbler does not have wing bars. Many bird books discuss and show a red crown patch but this is nearly impossible to see in the field. The back and tail of the warbler are an olive-green color common to this bird family.

Nests are neatly built of rootlets, grass, bark, and hair and generally are on the ground. The nests are concealed in moss or lichens with a canopy formed by a bush or plant near the site. It is almost always necessary to flush the incubating female in order to locate the nest. The male stays nearby singing his two-part *seebit-seebit-titititi* song. The female sticks closely to her task of warming the four or five creamy white eggs which are colored with a wreath of brown spots concentrated near the heavy end of the shell. The young hatch after only 11 or 12 days of incubation.

Areas of undergrowth in the woods attract the Nashville Warblers but they also like to stick close to the forest edges. Because they love masses of moss for use in nest building, you can often spot them flying about in boggy areas. From the bogs, they fly to deciduous forests where they find flying insects and crawling larvae. It is common to see these birds climbing along a branch and searching on the undersides of leaves for some of their favorite foods.

Cowbirds seldom bother the nests of the Nashville Warblers, perhaps because the nests are so small and carefully hidden. Migration in the fall usually occurs in the first half of September when many other species are passing through. In September and October, the Nashvilles funnel together and move south through the Mississippi watershed to a winter home from the Texas Gulf Coast to Guatemala.

Key Natural History References: Forbush 1929, Bent 1953, Griscom 1957, Lawrence 1948.

Tennessee Warbler *Vermivora peregrina*

It is difficult to cite one outstanding characteristic of plumage or behavior that will help you identify this plainly marked bird. Tennessee Warbler males have a gray cap, dull white eye line, white eyebrow stripe, an olive-green back and a white breast. Females have the same features but with a lighter gray head and a trace of yellow on their underparts. It's easy to confuse this warbler with the vireos, but they are much more nervous and quick moving than vireos, and that sharp little pointed bill of the Tennessee Warbler is distinctive.

Tennessee Warblers arrive in our region in May, and a bit later in northern parts of the Great Lakes region, on their way to southern Canada, which is the primary nesting habitat. In the spring they may be attracted to the tops of tall trees to gather insects, but if you provide a bird bath at that time of year, you can attract them down to ground level where they're much easier to watch.

Their song is also distinctive, a sharp bright quality pouring forth as they sing what was admirably described by one bird specialist as "their two or three-parted warble of *ticka ticka ticka, swit swit, chew chew chew chew.*" It's much like the song of the Nashville Warbler, but more tirelessly repeated. In fact, you may tire of it long before they do.

Tennessee Warblers nest mainly in Canada, but also in the northern areas of Minnesota, Michigan, Wisconsin, and New England. Most Michigan residents, therefore, should look for this bird only during spring and fall migrations when Tennessees pass through on their way north or south.

Their nests are made of grass and are usually located at ground level in sphagnum moss or on a dry tussock, commonly in a growth of small conifers. Usually five or six white eggs spotted with brown are laid, well concealed because the Tennessee female builds a canopy over the nest as an added protection against intruders. The female sits like a stone on these tiny eggs for 11 or 12 days until the young hatch. Her mate then joins her to feed the young their diet of insects.

As the young begin to mature, there is more yellow on their breasts than seen in the parents. This is a point to watch for during the fall migrations as these birds head south in September. Their pattern of travel, in our region at least, seems to angle southwest to follow the Mississippi valley to the Gulf, and then to follow the Mexican Gulf shore into Central and South America for the winter.

Look for this nervous little warbler in May in southern Michigan and early June in the U.P. If you live along the Lake Superior drainage of Michigan or Wisconsin, you may see it at anytime during the nesting season. And remember that warbler numbers suffer great variations from year to year, so if you fail to see Tennessees one year, they may well prove abundant the following year.

Key Natural History References: Forbush 1929, Bent 1953, Bowdish and Philipp 1916.

Black-capped Chickadee *Parus atricapillus*

My wife has adopted this lively little creature as her favorite bird. The hardy Chickadee, lively in all kinds of weather, is one of the species you may see every day of the year throughout the Great Lakes region. This tiny, trusting dynamo weighs barely a penny's-worth and will sit on your hat if you aren't careful. My wife admires them because they are so gracious about waiting their turn to pick at feeder seeds. They don't seem to mind letting other birds eat first. Notice the long tail, black cap, black bib, white cheeks, and light, buffy sides of this winged acrobat.

Chickadees love trees, bushes, shrubs, and open woodlands. There they build homes in the natural holes of trees and posts. You may spot nests excavated in soft, decaying trees by pairs of these birds, who possess unusually sharp but stubby bills. The Chickadees may also inhabit your birdhouses. After choosing a site, they bring in hair, soft plant fibers, bits of animal fur, and feathers to line the cavity. Usually, the entrance hole is just large enough to allow the passage of only one Chickadee at a time—a construction that prevents predation and keeps out Cowbirds. The nests that I have seen in trees and posts had such tiny entrance holes that we had to reflect sunlight into the hole with a mirror to detect the number of eggs. The five to ten, typically six to eight eggs, are white and speckled with light brown spots. While the female incubates for 12 days, her mate brings her meals of insect and spider eggs. He serenades her by continually repeating his name, a clearly enunciated *chick-a-dee-dee-dee,* as he defends the area. The female often covers the eggs with a soft material she brings to the nest. Once hatched, the young may stay in the warmth of the nest for 16 days. When the fledglings emerge, they already possess the plumage of their parents and immediately begin to scurry about the nest tree in search of the insects which they love to eat. The Chickadees' ability to hang upside down from the tip or underside of the tiniest twigs enables them to find food missed by other bark gleaners.

Chickadees are noted for their friendliness. Many deer hunters tell about the fearless little black and white birds that come to sit on their hat, shoulder, or gun barrel as they wait quietly on a stump near a deer path. You can even tame Chickadees in your yard if you work at it. Once they adapt to your feeder, they become increasingly bold as you refill the hoppers with either black or striped sunflower seeds, which they love, plus suet which replaces bug-protein in winter months. Hold out a handful of seeds, stand motionless for a minute or two, and they may land on you. It's a great experience.

Chickadees range from Alaska and Newfoundland to New Mexico and North Carolina, and are seen everywhere in Michigan throughout the year.

Key Natural History References: Odum 1941 and 1942, Brewer 1961, Kluyver 1961.

American Redstart *Setophaga ruticilla*

Redstarts are natty, small, "sharp dressers" that will impress you with a showing of their outstanding colors as they flit about butterfly-like, spreading their tails and drooping their flashy wings. A black coat trimmed with salmon red on wings, tail, and chest makes up the garb of the male. Females have a white breast and olive brown backs with yellow patches on wings and tail. The adults are only five inches long, but their bright colors make up for their small size.

Redstarts are found all over our Great Lakes region, most commonly in northern lower Michigan and in the U.P., and their small size will require that you watch diligently to spot them. In May, these members of the warbler family arrive in the lakes states searching for nesting sites. Many nest south of us, some as far as Alabama and Georgia; others go as far north as the limits of tree growth in northern Canada. A crotch formed by several branches of a sugar maple, basswood, aspen, cherry, apple, or elm tree is an ideal location for a Redstart's home. The female constructs a neat, firm pocket-like nest of whatever is available, such as plant down, bark, grass, feathers, spider webs, and lichens. The nest may be as high as 30 feet up in a tree or as low as four feet above the ground, tucked into some protected part of shrubbery or forest undergrowth.

The female lays three to five, but usually four, gray or bluish-white eggs spotted with chocolate brown. Egg laying takes place from late May to mid July. She sits on the eggs 12 to 14 days, and some birders report having seen the male feed her while she is incubating. The babies are inclined to leave the nest after only eight or nine days, and they become sexually mature after one year. Only one brood is produced each year. Both parents provide the youngsters with their insect diet while in the nest.

Redstarts eat a wide variety of insects, including caterpillars, bugs, flies, moths, grasshoppers, beetles, and wasps. Sometimes they may add a few berries and seeds to their menu, but mostly it's insects for dinner.

The Redstart young quickly develop the color patterns of the adults, but the young males keep the yellow patches of youth until they return to us from their first winter home far to the south. Then, in their second summer, they gradually redden in color. Some Redstarts may linger all winter along our Gulf Coast, but most go to Mexico and tropical countries of Central America for the winter, some going as far south as Venezuela. Listen for the *zee-zee-zee-zee-zwee* of this perky warbler and try to add it to your backyard list, any time from May through August. By the end of September, most have departed from our Great Lakes region for warmer climes.

Key Natural History References: Forbush 1929, Griscom 1957, Bent 1953.

Female

Male

Brown Creeper *Certhia familiaris*

Brown streaks on its back blend perfectly with the bark of most trees hugged by the little Brown Creeper as it moves around and up the trunk searching for insects. This bird is about five inches long, and nearly half of its length is made up of its spade-like tail. There have been reports that the diminutive Creepers spread their wings slightly as they snuggle close against the tree bark to hide from a hawk. When I've held one in my hand for banding, I was amazed to see such a fragile body and such spindly legs. For their own safety, they had certainly better hide when any predator is in the area.

Watch these little birds fly to the base of a tree and proceed to follow a spiral path around and around as they methodically work their way toward the top. In spring they find a loose piece of bark jutting out on which a nest can be built. The nest is usually not placed more than 10-15 feet above ground, and is formed of bark shreds, feathers, and small twigs, its shape conforming to the shelf on which it is built. Apparently the female builds the nest herself, although the male assists by bringing nesting material to her. Half a dozen creamy white eggs are laid, the shells peppered with cinnamon brown spots.

The tiny parents take turns incubating the eggs for two weeks; young stay in the nest for another two weeks after hatching, and when they leave home they are ready to creep along the bark next to the nest. This creeping helps them wear their tail feathers into sharp points so they have a prop to hold themselves tight against the side of a tree. When September comes the young have fledged out and look like the adults in every respect.

I have never seen Brown Creepers upside down on a tree. I watch them carefully in my yard and after they reach a height of 40 feet or more they fly down to the base of another nearby tree. Up they creep again searching for the tiny insects that comprise most of their diet. Sometimes they become very friendly and have been known to alight on a trouser leg to see if any insects can be found there.

The song of the Brown Creeper is very faint and is uttered only in breeding season: *see-ti-wee-tu-wee* or *see-see-see-sisi-see*. Without this song these birds would be almost impossible to locate, since they blend so well with a tree that they look like a bit of moving bark. Their bills are delicate and thin, and curve downward; with such a pointed instrument the bird can easily probe the cracks in the bark of most trees. Their exploration of the tree trunk for insects is carried on in a careful, almost painstaking manner. Some Creepers tarry with us all winter, but most travel to warmer southern states for the months of November to April.

Key Natural History References: Bent 1948, Forbush 1929.

Brown Creeper   5 inches

Common Redpoll *Carduelis flammea*

These wiggly little winter visitors are unpredictable about their visits to our Great Lakes backyards, but when they do arrive, it's frequently in bunches. Watch for them to visit with a group of Pine Siskins. Smaller than House Sparrows, only about five inches long, Redpolls frequently travel in flocks looking for weed patches extending above the snow cover. They are confirmed seed eaters, and it is quite a sight to see groups of them crawling all over weed stems searching for food. Against the snowy landscape Common Redpolls stand out sharply, with bright red caps on their foreheads and black trim around their bills, as well as jet black chins. The uniquely marked chin is what sets this bird apart from all others. Their streaked gray-brown bodies resemble that of a finch; the males sport a pink breast. Frequently, they prove quite friendly and will often sit only a few feet away waiting for me to fill the feeders. Their favorite winter food appears to be niger, those expensive little black imported thistle seeds, but they also relish sunflower seeds.

Redpolls appear here in the Great Lakes region only during the winter, moving north to northern Canada for their breeding season, where they build nests six to eight feet above the ground in willow or conifer trees. The nest is soundly constructed of twigs, rootlets, moss and grass, and may include a few feathers of larger birds. The female lays four or five blue-green eggs colored with a few dark spots. She incubates the eggs for 11 or 12 days and then, after the young hatch, she does most of the food gathering for the family while the male hovers nearby. The nest is rather unkempt, but considering all the mothering and food gathering the little brood requires, it's apparently tidy enough.

Redpolls usually move about in open country in a restless fashion, one of the marks that helps identify them. While feeding in an open place they will not remain in one spot very long. However, in sheltered places this fearfulness disappears. Many birdwatchers with feeders report that Redpolls are much less likely to take flight if humans approach than birds of other species. A common winter visitor in the north, irregular but often numerous in the southern third of Michigan, Redpolls are a colorful and friendly addition to your backyard bird family. They usually move on quickly with the approach of spring, but will sometimes stay well into May if I keep my feeders well filled. The song of the Common Redpoll, a high trill followed by a rattling *chet-chet-chet,* is heard in flight. In Canada, during summer nesting, they're found in alders and birches, the seeds of these trees forming an important part of their diet. During the winter in our region, any of the common weed seeds provide enough energy to keep the Redpoll lively. They have been seen in winter as far south as Texas, Alabama, and Georgia, but generally stay north of the Mason-Dixon line.

Key Natural History References: Bent 1968, Peterson 1980.

Male

Female

Field Sparrow *Spizella pusilla*

Seldom will you see these little sparrows in urban backyards, though they do occur. Go to the country, however, and you'll see them in rural backyards, as well as open fields where they glean for grain and weed seeds. Note that they have a rusty crown, clear breast, and pinkish bill. The rust of the crown is more subdued than that of the Chipping Sparrow, and the lighter eye line is very indistinct. Their favorite perch is on tall weeds, bushes, and other vegetation that is higher than the grass in which they spend most of their time.

Male Field Sparrows come to the Great Lakes states in March or April to select a territory that they will defend with vigor. The females arrive about 15 days after the males, and the eager males may mate with the first female that comes along. The first nests of the summer commonly are placed on the ground and are made of weeds, grass, and hair. Later in summer the nests for the second brood may be built up to four feet above the ground, because by July the weeds and grass are much taller than they were in May. The female builds the nest alone as her mate patrols the territory, letting everyone know he rules the area by sending forth a flood of song.

The four eggs are off-white with a blue or green cast; small spots at the large end are a rich brown color. The female incubates them about 11 days, and after the young hatch they develop a lightly streaked plumage. Often the hatchlings crawl out of the nest before they can fly. For about a month the parents feed them, but the mother may leave early to start another nest and turn over the baby sitting task to the male.

Since the nests of Field Sparrows are built rather low to the ground, the danger of destruction by predators is great. The female's instinct to raise a family is strong, however, so she may build several nests if necessary. When not hunting food, the male sits just a short distance away, raising his voice in persistent song.

An outstanding characteristic of the Field Sparrow is its gentleness. It is seldom aggressive toward any other bird; it feeds good-humoredly in mixed flocks of its own and other species in fall and winter. It is frequently confused with Chipping and Tree Sparrows, with whom it is often found during migration time. But its chestnut cap is not as bright as that of the Chipping Sparrow, and the Tree Sparrow does not have the pink bill of the Field Sparrow.

Here in the Lower Peninsula you should find a Field Sparrow on every summer hike through the country. In the U.P. they are less common. They stay with us until September or October and then head south to the warmer climes of our central and Gulf states, where they are seen until they return in March to the Great Lakes region.

Key Natural History References: Bent 1968, Best 1977 and 1978, Crooks 1948.

American Goldfinch *Carduelis tristis*

"**W**ild canary" is another name for the American Goldfinch, and these common small finches do look much like the typical caged pet shop canary. In the warm season of the Great Lakes region, the brilliant yellow of the male is offset with a jaunty black cap and black and white wings. The female is a muted yellow and appears more olive drab than her brightly colored mate. In winter, the male's plumage pales to near that of the female, at which time it's hard to tell them apart. But as spring approaches, yellow spots appear on the male's dull plumage, then begin to spread and blossom, and by the time the days are sunny and warm he is once again his brilliant yellow and black self.

Goldfinches are small, an inch shorter in body length than a sparrow. They are a flocking bird, and we often see a dozen or more at our feeders. Sometimes they will stay with us all year long, too, so it's fun to watch their comings and goings and changes in coloration. Their favorite food is the black thistle seed called Niger, and they are remarkably adept at picking up a seed, popping it open, removing the tiny kernel, and spitting out the shucks.

Their flight includes frequent deep undulations, as though they enjoy a roller-coaster ride. Their song is a bright liquid trill that sounds like *per-chik-o-ree*, or *ti-dee-dy-dy*. They have an unusually long song season because nesting may take place any time from early July until mid-September, and sometimes involves two separate nestings. Generally, however, they nest in August, after various thistles mature

enough to provide the soft downy fibers they prefer for nests. Their nests may be located only a foot or two off the gound, or up to 40 feet or more high. Sometimes nests are made on a sturdy mullein or large thistle; more frequently they prefer a secure tree crotch to build their solid, well-built, even water-holding nests. Plant fibers and grasses are the main building materials.

The female lays four to six, but usually five, bluish white eggs and then sits on them for 12 to 14 days. She is a faithful tight sitter, but her task is made easier by the male as he devotedly and routinely brings her meals of seeds and insects. The male continues to feed his mate and young for a few days after the hatch, then both parents work 11 to 15 days rearing the young to flight size.

Many things about these little birds make them attractive as backyard guests, so if you haven't seen any in your area, set out some thistle seed in a separate small tree-hung planter that has several separate perches. Goldfinches are a vivacious and friendly bird; at the feeders they are attractively boisterous and, finally, they consume many harmful insects in the summer months. We really enjoy these little feathered guests, which over the years have become one of our favorite backyard species.

Key Natural History References: Nickell 1951, Stokes 1950, Bent 1968, Walkinshaw 1938 and 1939.

Male

Female

Winter

Marsh Wren *Cistothorus palustris*

This irrepressible little marsh dweller spends a busy summer in our state. It is a constant hunter of insects and spiders in the reeds of its small territory where it stays hidden from view much of the time. While the male busies himself building numerous nests, most of which are never used, the female produces two and occasionally three broods of three to eight young in one or another of those nests.

Throughout the summer the marsh rings with the enthusiastic, high-spirited singing of these birds. They are slightly larger than the familiar House Wren, about five inches from the tip of their long curved bill to the end of their perky little tail. The Marsh Wren, known earlier as the Long-billed Marsh Wren, is identified by a *long white eye stripe* and *broad stripes on its back*. Its upper parts are mostly brown while the undersides are a buffy white. The dark back stripes alternate between dark brown or black and white.

It cocks its tail forward and its head backward so abruptly when excited that the two seem almost to touch. Its song is a mixture of scraping, squeaking, bubbling and chattering often preceded by a faint buzz. The male keeps up the song while building a collection of nests, being quiet only when carrying nesting materials which interfere with singing. And as with nest building, singing often continues into the night.

The nests are compact coconut-shaped and tennisball-sized globes of interwoven reeds fastened—sometimes securely, sometimes loosely—to the stems of reeds about 15 inches above water. Occasionally the nests are in alders and willows. They are lined with cattail down and similar soft materials and are entered through an opening on the side. Each is a nicely crafted little bird house which would fit easily into cupped hands. The eggs are laid in only one nest; the others nearby are dummies, built possibly as a ruse to confuse predators or simply to consume the male's boundless energy. They may also be used for roosting.

Because of its shyness and over-water habitat, this wren is not commonly seen, but shows itself in flights of song when it flutters a few yards into the air before dropping suddenly out of sight into cattails and sedges. The flights are convincing exhibitions of the little bird's great energy and enthusiasm.

The species generally is gregarious and large numbers often nest in good-sized marshes where there is abundant tall vegetation. Finding these congregations of excited birds and their compact globe-like homes make hours of sloshing through marshland a small price to pay.

In late fall, Marsh Wrens depart for their winter range, which extends from the mid-Atlantic States westward to Mexico.

Key Natural History References:
Verner 1965, Kale 1965, Welter 1935.

Yellow Warbler *Dendroica petechia*

These brightly-colored little yellow birds, called canaries by some people, are the most widespread of the warbler family. Their breeding grounds extend from the Atlantic to the Pacific in both Canada and the United States, and from Northern Canada to the Gulf States and Mexico. They should not be confused with the American Goldfinch; both birds are yellow, but the goldfinch possesses more black on the wings, perhaps the most easily observable difference in the field.

Yellow Warblers keep their distance from dense forests. They prefer low growth along streams, swamps and lakes but will often nest near residential areas having such surroundings. For this reason you may see them at your window or in your backyard. The nest is a sturdy wind-safe structure placed in a crotch formed by upright branches. Building materials include milkweed fibers, grass, and the down of plants and weeds. The nests are built so tightly that some have been known to hold water—not good for babies in a rain.

The four or five eggs are grayish or bluish white with brown and gray spots. The female sits on her nest for 11 days to hatch her nestlings, during which time she will receive food from the generally attentive male. The young remain in the nest about two weeks and are fed by both parents. They feed their offspring plenty of protein-rich food. Insects that the birds seek out are tent caterpillars and the larvae of the gypsy moth. Cowbirds are famous for depositing one of their eggs in a Yellow Warbler nest, and after hatching such an egg the tiny yellow parents drive themselves crazy trying to feed what they believe is an oversize warbler baby.

The Yellow Warbler is a gentle bird and is one of the tiniest and calmest birds you're likely to encounter in the wild. They usually do not seem to mind the close approach of humans, and it's possible for birdwatchers to sit for hours within a few feet of these birds as they go about their business of nest building or feeding their family. They are as comfortable around cameras as they are people and are easy subjects for picture taking.

The song of this warbler is a bright, cheerful, very musical phrase of about eight notes. The song has so many variations it is usually the quality, rather than the notes themselves, that identify this bird. There are two forms most often heard: *see see see see tititi see,* or less commonly *weet weet weet weet tsee tsee.*

Migration begins in August, during which time the tiny birds fly south for a warm winter in Mexico, the West Indies, and South America. Look for this yellow delight throughout the Great Lakes states during breeding season and the summer months.

Key Natural History References: Forbush 1929, Bent 1953, Schrantz 1943.

Male

Female

Chimney Swift *Chaetura pelagica*

A sharp twittering overhead is what usually calls attention to this swift-flying acrobat. It dashes about, here with wings beating rapidly, there alternating with rapid, short glides. At times the wing strokes are so fast they appear to beat separately as this small sparrow-sized bird races about through the air, playing tag and dodging other swifts, and chattering endlessly. Although it is not a swallow, it is often confused with swallows, despite a short, stiff, rounded unswallow-like tail. Its stiff swept-back wings suggest an arrow shot from a bow, and the cylindrical shape of head, body and tail makes the Chimney Swift look for all the world like a small cigar flying around up there. The bird is sooty-black in color with a slightly lighter throat. It has a short wide bill adapted to catching insects on the wing. Unseen in flight but nevertheless remarkable are the stiff bristles at the end of each tail feather which help this bird cling to the inside of chimneys, where it roosts in sizable groups. Its only call, which it utters frequently in flight, is a sharp chipping or twittering.

The nest, often placed well down inside a chimney, is a simple semicircular ledge of small twigs glued together against the bricks with a gooey secretion of the bird's salivary glands. The bird uses its sharp strong beak to snap the twigs from ends of dead branches, and the nest size is increased as family size grows. The four to six young hatch from pure white eggs.

When seen in the open, the Chimney Swift is always on the wing, tipping from side to side with its wings beating like stiff little paddles. It feeds entirely on the wing, eating a diet of flying insects. It may fly uninterrupted for an hour before returning to a chimney or other perch to rest. Even this rest is noisy and active, as the Swifts jostle one another for position.

One of the most delightful performances of this bird occurs in spring and fall when huge flocks gather in the evening and prepare to roost for the night. Thousands wheel in huge circles amid a din of twittering calls. Gradually the flock takes on a funnel-like tornado shape, spreading out from its base which whirls around some large industrial or public building chimney. Then rather suddenly the birds at the lower end begin to disappear as the entire flock seems to be sucked gradually downward into the chimney. Finally all are silent as the chimney holds thousands of these mysterious little birds, each clinging to a tiny spot on the sooty bricks.

For many years the mystery of the Swift was heightened by man's lack of knowledge of where it spends the winter months. It was long known to migrate in flocks to the southern limits of the United States, but then it seemed to disappear. However, it does not dive into the mud to hibernate, as people once said. In recent years its wintering grounds in Peru have been discovered, and that's where most spend the winter.

Key Natural History References: Bent 1940, Dexter 1977, Fischer 1958.

Swamp Sparrow *Melospiza georgiana*

Finding Swamp Sparrows often means wet feet for the bird watcher. This bird is most easily and frequently found in places best reached by wading or by boat. Freshwater cattail marshes and brushy swamps are its favorite playgrounds.

This is a shy sparrow, stout and dark with a clear gray breast and cheeks, a white throat, and a reddish, chestnut cap and faintly streaked sides. The reddish cap and the marshy home are the best field marks of the adult. Much of the back and wings are chestnut-colored, streaked with black. Immature Swamp Sparrows are streaked, but lack the red crown. Plumage coloration in the mature birds is the same for both sexes. Its most similar species is the Chipping Sparrow, but that delicate little bird, common here in the summer, is much slimmer and has a distinctive white stripe over the eyes.

In its open marsh home, the Swamp Sparrow is a secretive bird which prefers to keep itself concealed from humans. There in the deep marsh growth it runs up and down reed stalks like a mouse, constantly in search of seeds and insects. The inhospitable undergrowth of coarse marsh grass wears away at the bird itself, often leaving it with tail feathers worn down by the rough surfaces of the grass. On its infrequent flights above the grass it can be identified by a pumping motion of its tail. Alarmed, it runs or flutters to tangled cover and quickly disappears. In its search for insects it imitates the wading hunt of the Sandpiper in picking its food off the water surface. Insects make up almost 90 percent of its food, the remainder being seeds.

The female Swamp Sparrow lays her four or five eggs in a nest built on tufts of grass which rise out of the water, but the nest is often placed so low there is danger of destruction by changing water levels. A few nests are destroyed in this way by high water, but low water all around tends to reduce the bird's nesting choices, so that's not a helpful option either.

The Swamp Sparrow's song is a trill similar to that of the Chipping Sparrow. It is a slow, strong *tweet-tweet-tweet-tweet* especially marked by its resonant sweetness, all carried in the same note so rapidly that it is almost a twitter. One writer describes it as having the ring of cut glass. The single call note is a metallic *chink*.

The Swamp Sparrow is a year-round resident of southern Great Lakes marsh areas, while haunting more northerly marshes from mid-April and May to October or November. Winter, however, finds the majority of this bird's members deep in swamps as far south as the Gulf of Mexico.

Key Natural History References: Bent 1968.

Swamp Sparrow   5-5¾ inches

Tree Swallow *Iridoprocne bicolor*

The earliest swallow to arrive here from the south is the Tree Swallow. Graceful flight in their pursuit of insects is an important clue when identifying these birds. Tree Swallows are the size of a Sparrow, but have thin, streamlined bodies to slice through the air more rapidly. Their backs are shiny blue-green and their breasts are white. They are often seen in marshy areas which have dead trees in standing water—they nest in the trees and cruise over the water for insects. Many Tree Swallows nest in man-made boxes, too. Their assistance in controlling insects is one good reason to set out homes for them.

Courtship usually takes place in flight. Bluebird and Purple Martin houses that are very popular with people are also popular with Tree Swallows, to the extent that the birds sometimes seem to prefer wooden boxes rather than more natural homes, even nesting in ill-made or partially destroyed houses that offer incomplete shelter. The nest is made of grass and invariably lined with feathers. The birds show a preference for white feathers, and sometimes arrange them so that the feather tips curl upward over the eggs. Four to six pure white eggs are laid and the female sits tightly on the nest. I have opened boxes and found that she would stay parked while I stroked her back; her mate would sail close to my head and keep up a nervous chatter. Only occasionally do the males share incubating duties. They will carry food to their sitting mates, although the females also leave the nest for brief periods during the day to find food for themselves. Both parents feed the young and remove excretory material from the nest. The males seldom stay in the nest at night. They will usually perch on top of the wooden houses for an hour or more after their mates have retired, not leaving for their own secure sleeping location until after darkness has fallen.

Baby tree swallows will remain in the nest from 16 to 24 days. When they leave, they usually leave for good—most do not return to the boxes once they have flown away. They are strong fliers even during their earliest efforts. Young Tree Swallows stay with us until September, but some leave a bit earlier, joining hundreds of fellow family members and commonly perching on wires along roadways, an aggregation that may include Barn Swallows, Purple Martins, Bank Swallows, and Tree Swallows. All seem to fly south together in loose groupings.

Swallows go to our southern states and Central America for the winter. I enjoy seeing them return in spring because they are so helpful in keeping insect pests under control, and because they readily accept the nesting quarters I provide. At twilight in summer, if you drive to a nearby lake, you will very likely see these bright little birds swooping across the surface, picking up their insect meals.

Key Natural History References:
Graber et al. 1972, Paynter 1954,
Chapman 1955, Kuerzi 1941.

Yellow-rumped or Myrtle Warbler

Dendroica coronata

Many years ago, this common bird was called the Yellow-rumped Warbler; then for a time it was known as the Myrtle. Now the official name is once again the Yellow-rumped Warbler. About a half dozen other warblers have a yellow rump, but this is the only yellow-rumped warbler with a white throat. The male of this species is a sharply dressed bird. Besides the yellow on its rear, the crown and flanks have the same color, contrasting with heavy black cheeks and black upper breast patch. The back is blue-gray, and white bars appear on the wings. The female is more brownish-beige above and whitish below, with some yellow on the throat, sides and rump. Dark streaks on the chest replace the solid black patch of the male. These vividly-colored birds are House Sparrow size, about six inches long.

In the early days of spring migration, the arrival of the Yellow-rumped Warbler is an excellent sign that winter has departed. The handsome males arrive first, conspicuously hopping about in shrubbery and undergrowth, fluffing their yellow feathers to attract prospective mates as soon as females move into breeding territory. Most Yellow-rumped Warblers that come our way continue north during spring migration to find coniferous woods on the northern borders of Minnesota, Wisconsin, Michigan, and other northern states, as well as much of Canada. Their song is a trill with loose, open rises or drops in pitch toward the end of the song. Also a *check, check* calling sound.

Nests are placed from 5 to 40 feet above ground, typically in a spruce or hemlock near the center of the tree. They are a neat composition of twigs, bark, plant down, and feathers, built with an arch over the eggs. When the female leaves the nest for food, the arch helps protect the exposed eggs.

The female incubates three to five, typically four, eggs for 12 or 13 days. They are cream to white in color with a brown and gray speckled wreath shading the thick end. The young birds have a brown down covering at first, and may leave the nest early to creep about on nearby branches of the conifer. In the fall, when the birds start their migration south, the offspring still have a brownish cast over the dark areas of their bodies.

Yellow-rumped Warblers eat lots of insects, but supplement their diet in winter with the fruits of bayberry and juniper bushes, the red cedar, and other plants such as poison ivy, woodbine, honeysuckle and mountain ash. Beetles and flies are their favorite insects. A few members of this species spend the winter with us in the southern portions of the Great Lakes states (it is the only warbler seen regularly during the cold months in Michigan), but most leave in October to winter in our southern states and south to Panama.

Key Natural History References: Forbush 1929, Morse 1976, Bent 1953, MacArthur 1958.

Male

Female

Song Sparrow *Melospiza melodia*

All across the lower 48 states, Song Sparrows notify you of their presence with their loud and frequent singing. The song contains 7 to 11 notes and varies up and down in pitch, includes trills, and comes pouring forth at the rate of 5 or 6 per minute. Their brownish back is quite sparrow-like, and their white breast is streaked with brown. A central brown spot below the throat is perched there like a tie-pin. Song Sparrows move their rounded tail rhythmically as they fly. Spaces near water bordered by light vegetation are preferred by this species; look for them in willows and bushes that line a lake or marsh. The nest is placed on the ground next to a body of water, or if not there, it will be found low in a shrub hanging over the water.

The males arrive in our region early in the spring to start singing and to establish territories. The male song usually starts with three or four bright repetitious notes: *sweet sweet sweet sweet,* then continues into trills and warbles as noted above. When the females arrive, soon after, mating takes place and the female begins to build the nest, a neat cup-like structure of grass and weed stems. One day we found a nest perched in a sturdy weed about three feet above the edge of a pond; inside four brownish eggs lay together in the well built home. When we returned a few days later all the eggs had disappeared; apparently some predator had taken them. This happens to many Song Sparrow nests because they are placed close to the ground and so are available to predators. However, if the female can maintain the nest for about two weeks, she will hatch young which are then fed by both sexes. Her urge to continue nesting is strong, so she may fly off soon after and start another nest. She usually lays three to six pale brown or green eggs in each nesting, each heavily spotted with reddish brown. Some summers she may raise three broods; this provides a buffer so the species can withstand the toll of predation. Besides a variety of predators, the Cowbird is also an enemy of the Song Sparrow and frequently invades the nest. See the Cowbird essay in this book for more on this interesting habit.

Although Song Sparrows prefer low, wet land—the banks of streams, the bushy shores of ponds, shrubby wet meadows or cattail swamps—they can be found over a wide range of conditions, even rocky wooded clearings at high altitudes. They are furtive in the wild, and will usually run like a mouse from a pursuer rather than fly away. But Song Sparrows that dwell near humans often become quite tame. They come to bathe every night just after sunset if water is available.

On summer field trips it's often possible to find Song Sparrows because of their constant singing and their high numbers. In January look for them along areas of water that stay open all year. The birds that do leave us migrate to milder weather in the states just south of us, though some go as far south as Mexico.

Key Natural History References: Nice 1937, Nice 1943, Bent 1968.

5-6½ inches

Alder, Willow and Least Flycatchers

Empidonax alnorum, Empidonax traillii, Empidonax minimus

These are three of Michigan's most confusing birds, because they look so much alike only an expert can tell them apart in the field. And often, even with the bird in hand, calling one the Alder, another the Willow, and the third Least is done with no little uncertainty.

They are all small, 5¼ to 5½ inches in body length, with dark olive-brown backs and light breasts washed slightly with gray, buff, or yellow. They have short tails, light eye-rings, and two white wing bars, and they share a common habit of flipping their tails up and down as they perch. The Least may be a bit grayer above and whiter below, but only slightly so, and these are not reliable differences in the field. Their similarities are so great that until recent years the Willow Flycatcher was considered a subspecies of the Alder and both were known as the Trail's Flycatcher.

The identification is further complicated by the fact that we have similar species in the Great Lakes region with relatively minor identifiable differences—the Wood Pewee for one, which looks the same except for the absence of an eye ring. The Yellow-bellied Flycatcher, also similar, is told from the others only by a slight yellowish tinge to its underparts.

In observing all these Flycatchers it is probably safest to lump them into their genus name *Empidonax*, especially in the spring during migration. "I saw an Empidonax Flycatcher this morning" is a more believable statement among birdwatchers than using a specific name. Voice and habitat are the best means of separating species, and then only in the breeding season. The Least Flycatcher's call, for example is a vigorous *che-bek!* emphasizing the second syllable. It is given with a head jerk and tail twitch as often as sixty times a minute during courtship. The Least prefers open groves and orchards for its habitat, as well as open woodlands relatively free of growth under the forest canopy.

The Alder Flycatcher on the other hand prefers to flit about in slashings and willow and alder thickets on the edges of streams and swamps, though it also is found in scrubby pastures. Generally the environment is moist. Its call is a descending *fee-bee-o*.

The Willow Flycatcher is found most often on willow-covered islands and in shrubbery near water or near beaver meadows. Its call, which seems to some to say *"free beer,"* and *"fitz-bew"* is equally high pitched and accented.

Alder Flycatchers nest in bushes only a few feet above the ground, while the Willow and Least Flycatchers nest higher in both deciduous and coniferous trees. All the nests are small, typically three inches in diameter or less. Four eggs are commonly laid.

In the fall these three Flycatchers leave Michigan's confused birdwatchers behind and migrate to winter grounds in Central and South America.

Key Natural History References: Bent 1942, Breckenridge 1956, Graber et al. 1974, King 1955, MacQueen 1950, Stein 1958, Walkinshaw 1966 b.

Least Flycatcher   5¼ inches
Alder Flycatcher   5½ inches
Willow Flycatcher   5½ inches

Alder/Willow

Least

Chipping Sparrow *Spizella passerina*

Rusty-crowned sparrows that you see in summer are chippers. The clear white eye lines, the black line through the eye, and the unstreaked breast help you to identify these friendly little characters. They like to live near people and nest in many backyards where barberry and yews will provide nesting sites; the territory of a pair may include several yards and the male defends them well. The song is a series of sounds on one pitch, uttered all day long in breeding season—a dry *chip*.

Nests of the chipper are snug, built by the female out of grass, rootlets, and weed stalks, which are then lined with hair. Many birders say the nests are generally placed about 15 feet above ground but I believe just as many are placed only two or three feet above the ground. Chippers love to build in landscaping bushes, in old orchards, and in coniferous trees; nests are neatly tailored into a circular cup which is securely anchored to branches near the nest.

Four pretty blue eggs with brown spots are laid, and too frequently the larger speckled white eggs of the Cowbird are found in a chipper's nest as well. If you discover such a batch be sure to carefully remove and destroy the large Cowbird egg. The female Chipping Sparrow lays one egg daily early in the morning before she sits down to incubate the entire clutch, with the male bringing her food between his singing sessions. Sometimes he twitters a bit to alert her that he is approaching, probably because she sits tight and could be alarmed by a sudden approach. In a couple of weeks the eggs hatch, and the young, highly streaked on the breast in contrast to the parents, are fed by both parents. For about two months the young retain this streaked plumage, gradually changing after that into the adult coloration.

Chipping Sparrows eat lots of insects in summertime but over a whole year are predominantly seed eaters. Watch them as they search for seeds on your lawn—maybe they'll remove crabgrass seeds in the process. As a group, they are friendly and inhabit many green yards throughout the Great Lakes region all summer. They are fun to watch in flight, as they will occasionally lunge after a flying insect in flycatcher fashion. Also they seem to enjoy roughhousing in the air; usually just two but sometimes more of these sparrows will engage in brief, aerial combats—complete with excited calls and agile maneuvers—for seemingly no reason at all. They raise two broods of young each summer, which is fortunate because they have lots of enemies such as Cowbirds, cats, snakes, and squirrels. If you retreat to Florida in the winter months watch for Chippers in that locale. They also winter in other Gulf states, and south into Mexico.

Key National History References:
Walkinshaw 1944, Bent 1968, Forbush 1929.

Indigo Bunting *Passerina cyanea*

The high-pitched song and brilliant blue color of this bird will be sure to capture your attention. The male's loud persistent song of *sweet-sweet* or *tsick-tsick* during nesting season is usually rendered from a high perch on the uppermost branch of a tall maple, oak, or hickory tree, or on some nearby utility wires. The birds usually choose to live on the edge of woods because they enjoy open space for roaming. In spring the male's plumage shines bright blue, but in the fall his plumage molts and he then resembles the predominantly dull, brown female, who has just faint brushes of blue on her wings and tail. The female can be distinguished from a sparrow by her unstreaked back. Occasionally, though not often, suburban or rural residents will see this bird in their backyards. Usually it stays in heavier cover or high in trees, but we've included it here so you won't be caught unawares if it does turn up one day.

After mating occurs, the female builds her nest in a bush, perhaps only three feet above the ground. A meticulous builder, she is fussy about the material she uses, constructing a solid nest of rootlets, grass, leaves, and other special items she may find, such as a papery snakeskin. She lays two to six, typically three or four, unspotted eggs and manages all the incubation work herself while the male sings from a lofty spot in a nearby tree. After 12 or 13 days the young emerge from the eggs and start life with a high-protein insect diet provided by both parents. The Bunting pair, which may produce a second brood by summer's end, is an easy target for the Cowbird, which will lay one or more of its eggs in the Bunting nest, which the adult Buntings then raise—to the detriment of their own young. See the essay on the Brown-headed Cowbird in this book for more discussion of this parasitic habit.

It is an occasional treat to see the bright blue males hopping about on a country road, because they like open areas where they can forage for stony grit for their food grinding crops. They also find weed seeds in abundance along roadways, so watch for these flashes of blue as you travel. The rich, iridescent blue of the male is so unique and appealing you will have no difficulty identifying him. His lively song rings out again and again during nesting season and he's a conspicuous singer at midday, so be sure to look and listen for him every summer.

In the fall, this fascinating little bunting departs for Costa Rica, Honduras, and other warm Central American countries. When spring returns, so will these tiny charmers. This small version of a Blue Grosbeak breeds from North Dakota and New Brunswick to Texas and Georgia, and can be seen in both the Upper and Lower Peninsulas of Michigan, although it's less common in the U.P.

Key Natural History References:
Bradley 1948, Allen 1936, Bent 1968.

Female

Male

Purple Finch *Carpodacus purpureus*

Although purple is one of the most brilliant colors in all of nature, it is not really the color of the male Purple Finch. He has a more reddish tone—like having had raspberry juice splashed on every feather. The female, as is the case with many species in the bird kingdom, doesn't share her mate's bright plumage; she has the mouse-gray color of the English Sparrow, with a streaked breast and a light eye line. Both sexes are about sparrow size. The male, however, does not show his magnificent color until more than a year old.

The courtship behavior of these birds is intense and colorful. The male flutters upward to perform an aerial dance for the watching female, singing his high-pitched warble as he goes. This practice may be seen throughout the nesting range, which includes the upper two-thirds of Michigan, the entire northern tier of states, and all of southern Canada. After mating, the male leaves the female to build the nest alone. She's a careful builder, pulling together fine rootlets and small twigs to form a cup-shaped nest tucked about 15 to 20 feet up in a young evergreen. Usually four bluish-green eggs are laid, marked with just a few dark spots. The female alone incubates the eggs for about 13 days in the well built nest, which is usually concealed securely among evergreen needles.

But this secretive habit only appears during nesting because Purple Finches are gregarious birds, especially in winter. They are usually sociable and friendly except when competing for food, when they seem quite reluctant to share their bounty with neighbors.

Birds already munching on seeds often are hostile to new arrivals, often raising their crown feathers and rushing at the newcomer with open beaks. Occasionally a peck or two will be exchanged, but the usual result is that the newcomer retreats out of range.

Sunbathing, common among Robins and a few other birds, is sometimes indulged by Purple Finches. At such times they occasionally assume strange, almost contorted postures with feathers fluffed and wings outspread, in obvious delight that the warm sun is flooding throughout their bodies.

The song of this bird is loud, clear, and musical—a fast, lively warble. The call note is a short, sharp *tick*. The best time to listen for Purple Finches is from late February or early March to July.

In winter their range extends from the Canadian border to the Gulf states. In order to attract these pretty birds to your feeder, make sure plenty of seeds are set out, since an adult's diet is almost 100 percent vegetable matter. Purple Finches are truly a brilliant and welcome sight at feeders, and they never fail to cheer us on those dragged-out days of a long winter.

Key Natural History References: Bent 1968, Pough 1949.

Male

Female

"Slate-colored" or Northern Junco

Junco hyemalis

"**S**nowbird" is the name many people give to these little sparrow-sized birds with gray backs and white breasts. When they take flight from your feeder or the side of the road you'll notice obvious white feathers along the edges of their tails.

This Junco nests in northern Michigan, and throughout the upper Great Lakes region. However, residents of southern Michigan should begin to look for them in October when they shift from Canada to our more southern counties. Most Juncos will stay with us until April or May. With their whitish bills, Juncos scour the ground below every feeder to salvage anything thrown aside by other birds; as they move they continually peck at each dark spot they see on the snow. Usually several can be seen together searching in this way, being quite social in their habits.

Anyone spending any time in the north woods of Michigan, Wisconsin, Minnesota, and Canada in summer will frequently see these little members of the sparrow family. Nests are located on sites chosen by a pair of birds very early in the season. They are built on the ground by the female; she makes the cup of twigs, bark, hair, and other material that she and her mate haul to the nesting site. Nests are usually placed under an overhanging plant on the side of a hill or beneath a frond of a bracken fern. During nesting season, the call of this bird is often heard, a light ticking, clicking sound, while its song is more of a trill, and a set of sounds that I find quite musical.

The four or five eggs are grayish or bluish white with brown spots at the wider end. The female incubates them about 12 days and has the assistance of her mate when it's time to feed the young family. Many caterpillars are converted into growing Juncos at this time and the parents work diligently to keep the nest in a sanitary condition. At 11 or 12 days of age the brown-backed young leave home, but continue to depend on the parents for food for several weeks.

In summer Juncos thrive on insects; in fall and winter, seeds become the major portion of their diet. When a thin layer of snow lies on the ground, a Junco will scratch at an area by hopping forward and then back with both feet at once until a space three or four inches in diameter is cleared. Then, if another Junco hasn't quickly invaded the site, the little gleaner will peck at the exposed seeds or grain with its pale bill.

These tiny snowbirds are one of our earliest arrivals in the fall and serve to tell us that the year-end holidays will soon be with us. Every winter we have some of these birds visit us, but the number varies up or down depending on the severity of the weather. More snow seems to bring more "Snowbirds," a fact we don't mind at all. Watch for these quick, soft-colored birds with the plain white outer tail feathers, and remember that if you see one you will probably see several more.

Key Natural History References: Bent 1968, Fretwell 1969, Forbush 1929.

House or "English" Sparrow

Passer domesticus

Many people can readily identify sparrows, but aren't sure which is which because of many similarities in the diversity of sparrow types native to our region. The House or "English" Sparrow, however, is really a Weaver Finch, not a sparrow, and is the one usually referred to as "just another sparrow."

The first arrivals came from England and were released in Central Park, New York City, in 1853 by Eugene Scheifflin, a wealthy drug manufacturer who wanted America to have every bird mentioned in all of Shakespeare's plays. Scheifflin also released the Starling, a move that in itself produced so much concern that congress soon passed restrictions on any future importations. Scheifflin's Weaver Finch, our "sparrow," has since spread to every corner of our land. Some observers say that the number of these birds has declined as the horse population has declined. But now that horses are returning, we hope these "sparrows" keep their population under control. They are, for many, still too numerous.

The male House Sparrow is rather attractive if you see the black bib and gray crown of a clean specimen. If anything, the female is more drab than the male but both sexes are aggressive, even brazen in their behavior and will attack any other species their size, plus some that are larger. They are tough little street fighters. Nests are built as a joint effort by the male and female in every location imaginable—eaves, martin houses, drain pipes, garage rafters, and many other available sites. Because of the boldness of these birds,

many other species lose their nesting sites to the House Sparrow. Their nests, for a small bird, are bulky, and made of grass, weeds, twigs, bits of paper, and anything soft that comes to use. Usually five eggs are laid and several nestings may occur each summer; the eggs are white to greenish with some brown spots. The female incubates them for 12 to 13 days.

The House Sparrow is primarily a seed and vegetable eater, and inhabits towns and cities throughout the lower 48 states. The song of this bird is a simple chirp, uttered repeatedly. Your feeders may be monopolized by House Sparrows because of their numbers and aggressive behavior. If so, try taking in all bird foods for a time till they stop coming. Some birdwatchers, both urban and rural, report no Sparrows at all, while others report seeing only an occasional visitor. In small numbers, these sturdy little birds add to our local scene; it's only when they drive away all other birds by their great numbers that we become concerned. Lovers of Martins and of Bluebirds are especially active in trying to keep House Sparrow populations down to a reasonable level.

This bird is a year around resident throughout the Great Lakes region.

Key Natural History References:
North 1972, Summers-Smith 1958,
Weaver 1942.

Male

Female

Ovenbird *Seiurus aurocapillus*

This heavy-bodied little warbler of the forest floor is sometimes dubbed "The Teacher Bird," because of its *teacher, Teacher, TEACHER* song, which grows more emphatic and louder toward the end—like a teacher no student hears. But it also has a fascinating flight song which is a real jumble of notes of several pitches high and low, mixed with warbles and twitters and *teachers*. If you find yourself in a mature woodlot with an open floor, watch for, and listen for this delightful song.

Ovenbirds are more often heard than seen, but if you have thick woods near your home, you may expect to find them resident nearby throughout the Great Lakes region all summer long. They can be mistaken for sparrows, but a couple of distinguishing marks will help you: First, they have pinkish legs, unlike any of the sparrows; and second, they have an orange-brown crown patch, bordered in black. Most of their feeding is done on the forest floor, but they like to perch on low limbs while they sing.

Ovenbirds move into our area about mid-April. Nesting occurs in a large territory from Georgia to the provinces of Canada. Nests are built of grass, pine needles, leaves, and rootlets in a small depression on the ground; a roof of weeds and stems makes the nest look like a little oven. It is usually so well hidden under leaves and other debris that you will probably not be able to see it, and a major problem is how to avoid stepping on it. The birds usually walk, not fly, to the location of the nest. Ovenbird eggs have a white shell decorated with a brown wreath on one end; there are usually four or five of them. The female incubates for 12 or 13 days and during this period will not flush easily. When we have found the nest of an Ovenbird it was because we noticed the bird sneaking through the grass some distance from the nest.

The male helps feed the chicks and usually brings his provisions on foot when he nears the area of the covered structure. Predators such as snakes and raccoons destroy many nestlings, and Cowbirds frequently make a deposit in the nest. The rich protein diet of the Ovenbird includes insects, snails, slugs, and earthworms harvested from the forest floor. The young may move out from the nest when only eight days old, but they do not fly for several more days.

By the time of fall migration the young have the plumage of an adult. Waves of Ovenbirds fly south and most of them leave the United States, the West Indies and South America providing winter homes for the majority from November to March. A few, however, refuse to fly across the Gulf, so they occasionally are seen wintering along our Gulf Coast.

Key Natural History References: Forbush 1929, Bent 1953, Hann 1937.

Red-eyed Vireo *Vireo olivaceus*

We treasure our remaining forests and so does the Red-eyed Vireo, one of the most common birds of the tall trees. This bird is House Sparrow size—six inches—and has a gray cap, contrasting with an olive-green back, a white breast and a distinct black-bordered white eyebrow stripe. The Vireo's brief monotonous robin-like song is uttered over and over again in courting and nesting season. These shy birds move about constantly, and diligent searching is needed to get a good view of them in the large deciduous trees they favor.

As the leaves are unfolding in the springtime, the Vireo comes to our lakes region from South America. Upon arrival, the birds get busy scouring leaves and tree bark to find the tiny worms and insects they relish. The pesky tent caterpillars which infest our trees are a delicacy that we are happy to give to the Vireos.

The nests of the Red-eyed Vireo are a sight you will enjoy—if you can find one. The female builds her neat cup in less than a week's time. The compact egg receptacle hangs below the fork of a branch and typically is placed 10 feet or more above ground level in a tree well concealed by foliage. The nest is constructed of fine grasses, bits of bark and rootlets, and is securely attached to the branch with fine spider webbing. The outside of the nest frequently is finished with a coating of lichens. In this compact cup the female lays three or four white eggs spotted with russet; she sits on them for two weeks.

Babies growing in the nest are nurtured with rich protein larvae and insects. After the young leave the nest, they pester their parents for food for several weeks. The mother may be warming a new brood by this time and appears annoyed at the demands the young make of her. The young feather out during the summer so they look like their parents when September arrives. Only the brown eye of the juvenile reveals its youth, the color not changing until its second year of life. However, neither the red eye of the adult, nor the brown eye of the young is distinct from a distance, so the observer can't depend on this for long-range identification.

Cowbirds are a real nuisance to the Red-eyed Vireo. In some areas, 80 to 90 percent of the Vireo nests possess one or more Cowbird eggs. Throughout the summer Vireos continue to scramble about in their forest home, and without doubt they assist in controlling insect infestations of our forests. Occasionally you will find them hustling about in the thick undergrowth of the woods. When fall comes, they take flight to South America, but once the snow melts, they return and are found in all states east of the Rockies.

Key Natural History References: James 1976, Lawrence 1953, Williamson 1971, Bent 1950, Southern 1958.

Tufted Titmouse *Parus bicolor*

Several years ago I watched a titmouse sneak behind a fox squirrel and suddenly peck at his tail. At that time I attributed this behavior to the fact that this is a mischievous bird; now I realize that this sassy little fellow was gathering hair for its nest. I still see this gray and white bird with the flesh-colored sides as a brash character who takes a back seat to no one. The titmouse is sparrow size, has unusually bright eyes, and sports a perky tuft on the top of its head. The sexes look alike. When a Cooper's Hawk visited our yard one winter all the birds froze except a brazen titmouse, which took flight and escaped into the woods when the hawk gave chase.

Titmice seem to be family oriented; if one individual comes into the feeder, invariably two or three more will soon put in their appearance. In nesting season it is common to hear a family of three or four young screaming at the parents to bring some food. Every summer I band many young ones that still have the light-colored flanges on the sides of their bills, and they are noisy and wiggly as I place the tiny aluminum bands on their legs.

Titmice are residents of the Lower Peninsula all year and can be heard singing their short song on bright days in February. In courting season they repeatedly call to their mates, and I have frequently imitated their song to produce a response from them: *peter, peter, peter,* or *here, here, here* in a clear whistled chant.

Nests are built in natural cavities of trees, old woodpecker holes, and in birdhouses. Leaves, grass, string, and hair are brought in to make a nest cup.

After five or six lightly spotted white eggs are laid, the female incubates them for two weeks. While sitting, she is fed by the male, and some bird watchers have noticed that the male calls to her and she comes out to pick up her meal. Babies stay in the nest for two weeks, and the family moves about as a unit for several weeks after the young fledge out and leave the nest.

The diet of Tufted Titmice is more animal than vegetable with quantities of insects being consumed. However, they love to feast on sunflower seeds; the protein of these seeds is so substantial they can serve as animal-type food. When they come to the feeder, titmice do not park for five minutes while they consume seeds; each bird flies in to find the supply of seeds, quickly grabs one, then scurries to a branch of a tree a short distance away. There they grasp the seed with their claws, hold it tight against the branch, and pound it open with their bill. The tiny kernel is extracted and the titmouse rushes back for another morsel. It almost seems as if all the energy used to get one seed doesn't equal the energy gained from the seed. In any case, every feeder needs a few of these active, perky little birds to brighten the day.

Key Natural History References: Gillespie 1930, Bent 1946, Forbush 1929, Laskey 1957, Boyd 1962.

Eastern Wood Pewee *Contopus virens*

Eastern Wood Pewees have gray-brown backs , a whitish breast, and two white wing bars, which are the only ways you can tell this bird from the Eastern Phoebe, which it resembles closely. The lower mandible of the Pewee is flesh-colored and the bird is about sparrow size. The Pewee does not usually wag its tail like the Phoebe, but has the flycatcher habit of sitting on dead branches and exploding out a short distance to catch an insect that flies by. Their nests are much different than the Phoebe's and typically are located in sites hidden in trees.

Wood Pewees are obscurely marked, small flycatchers. They love to sit high in branches, usually in thick woods, so that for the most part they are hard to find. Usually a birder finds one by first hearing its call and using this vocal clue to narrow the field of search. To add to the difficulty, this bird is a bit of a recluse. There is none of the aggressiveness that marks the behavior of some of the larger flycatchers, and a Wood Pewee is almost invariably alone or in the company only of its mate or its young.

Pewees say their name when they sing, but they use three syllables to do it: *pee-a-wee*, the last note a little lower pitched than the first one. Nests are flat like a small saucer and placed well out on a tree limb. It appears that Wood Pewees become attached to a certain group of trees, and birds believed to be of the same family group apparently return year after year to build their nest in the same tree, even on the same branch. Twigs and rootlets make the body of the nest, and the outer coating is a layer of lichens. Eggs are usually three in number and are creamy white with a brown wreath on the wider end of the egg. The female keeps the eggs warm for 13 days all by herself, while the male defends the area with great vigor and determination.

Both parents feed the young quickly but quietly, so as not to reveal the nest site. When the young fly out of the little saucer they have yellowish breasts. I've watched a family of them at the birdbath; they sit on a stump behind the bath and fly into the water as though they are chasing insects—they just bang into the surface. It seems a bit more like Olympic diving than bathing.

The birder's first encounter with the Pewee will perhaps be confusing; the wing bars, the light-colored lower mandible, and the lack of eye-rings seen in the Least and Alder Flycatcher group will help in identification. Also, the flycatchers, including the Pewee, all behave in a similar manner, so you can soon put them in the right family. The song of the Pewee is distinctive, after the observer has heard it uttered several times. Wood Pewees are common throughout Michigan in the warm season, but at the conclusion of summer these little flycatchers depart for Central and South America to thrive on the myriads of insects found there.

Key Natural History References:
Graber et al. 1974, Bent 1942,
Johnston 1971.

American Tree Sparrow *Spizella arborea*

American Tree Sparrows are among the most abundant winter residents of the north central United States. They have a creamy-white breast with a central dark spot, while their bill has a dark upper part and a light yellow lower part. "Tree" sparrows are misnamed, for few birds spend less time in trees than these little ones. They might more accurately be called "Brush" sparrows, for they are usually found near or on the ground on the scrubby edges of fields and marshes. Usually they will be in flocks of varying sizes and will visit us quite regularly in the winter months. Feeders in somewhat open areas will attract these sparrows better than feeders placed in deep woods.

After spending winter with us the tree sparrows gather in large flocks and move to the brushy areas of northern Canada that are just south of the tundra. There a home site is chosen and the female builds a sturdy nest under a clump of moss or grass; she incorporates grass, weeds, bark, and moss in the structure, and feathers are commonly included, sometimes from the white Arctic Ptarmigan. During her construction work the male defends the territory with his incessant singing. When the nest is completed, the female lays three to five bluish-white eggs speckled with brown. She must sit on the eggs without respite to protect them from the chill Arctic summer, and is able to move about only after the young hatch. The young are inclined to leave the nest rather early, before they can fly, but the parents follow them about and continue their caring ways until flight is possible. Even after flight begins, the family continues as a group until migration southward starts in the fall.

About six weeks after hatching, the young have feathered out to look similar to their parents, though duller brown and streaked dusky above and below. The main food of the American Tree Sparrow is seeds, which makes them good prospects to attract to your feeder. They also love weed seeds and will chatter endlessly as a group while gleaning their food from dried weeds in open fields. You may observe them jumping from ground level to weed tops at such times throughout our winter months. In our area that means they must thrive on plants that stand taller than the deep snow; perhaps this is done to show us that they have overcome their worst enemy—snow—which kills many in breeding season when late storms bury the nests. So look for this winter "chippy" at your feeders in the cold, wintry months only; they will be long gone to the far north as soon as the spring daylight begins to lengthen—signalling time once again to head north to the nesting grounds.

Key Natural History References: Bent 1968.

Barn Swallow *Hirundo rustica*

Barns are decreasing in number, so the Barn Swallow is trying to adapt to new places to build its nests. Look under bridges, along a rocky cliff, or in some cranny on modern houses; another good spot is along the piers or boat docks on the shore of a lake. Their mud nests are attached skillfully to beams, rafters, or trusses in many buildings. These birds carry on a continual chatter as they fly around the nesting areas, but are especially active in the waning hours of the day. When they nest in barns it is really amazing to watch them sail full speed into a barn with its many open doors, windows and cracks; if you see a bird do this it will be one with a rust-colored breast, a steel blue back, and a deeply forked tail. This is the only swallow in our area that is truly swallow tailed. The body of the bird is a little longer than a sparrow's.

In a dry spring, it is wise to make some muddy patches if you have a barn in the immediate vicinity, because the nest is constructed of mud pellets that both sexes carry in their bills to the building site. If the nest is placed on the side of a rafter it will be a half cup, with straw and feathers lining the inside. The eggs are six small creamy white homes for the embryos, with brown spots decorating the entire egg. Both sexes incubate, changing shifts frequently during the day, the female sitting on the nest at night with the male nearby. Fifteen days of incubation and 18 days of baby growth means more than a month of work for the parents. Often two broods are raised each summer, and the young with their lighter breasts usually far outnumber the adults by the end of the nesting season.

Flies are the main diet item, and cows and other livestock usually associated with a barn enjoy the help these birds provide in fighting the myriads of flies. The birds sail about gobbling up as many flies as they can catch. Occasionally they may play a game of catch with a feather before it is brought to the nest. When 30 or 40 pairs of Barn Swallows use the same barn for a home, the chatter of all of them makes quite a din in the evening. If you do not have this bird on your list, and want to see one, stop at a farm with a large barn and you will almost surely see some members of this lively tribe.

In August the Barn Swallows, Bank Swallows, Cliff Swallows, and Purple Martins perch together along telephone wires in rural areas and chatter endlessly about migration plans. Check a line-up of this kind to see which birds are present. Soon they will depart for Mexico and points farther south to escape wintry weather of the Great Lakes states.

Key Natural History References: Samuel 1971, Graber et al. 1972, Bent 1942, Davis 1937.

Bobolink *Dolichonyx oryzivorus*

The Bobolink is occasionally seen in backyard shrubbery, though more commonly it is a bird of the open fields and could have been included in the companion *'Coat Pocket Bird Book'* as readily as here. In spring the male is the only song bird that is solid black below and mostly white above, suggesting a dress suit on backwards. In autumn they resemble a House Sparrow, sporting a rich buff coloration with dark stripings on the crown and back.

The male is strikingly handsome and full of song. Thoreau described him as "this flashing, tinkling meteor [which] bursts through the expectant meadow air, leaving a train of tinkling notes behind." His song is enthusiastic and bubbling, starting with low, reedy notes and trilling upward.

Each spring when the Bobolink returns on its long flight from South America, it seeks out its favorite environment, a hayfield. When the male finds a field which suits him, he sets up a territory and waits for the later arriving females.

After courtship and mating, the nest is built, well hidden in a depression on the ground. The female is very watchful when she is brooding, constantly stretching her neck in order to peer over or through the concealing vegetation that surrounds her nest. She does the incubation while the male sings from his perch on the tallest weed he can find in the area. And when the five or six eggs are hatched, he helps to care for the young. Both parents feed the growing chicks an endless supply of insects and seeds. When alarmed, the parents leave the nest and move away quietly through the grass before they fly, making the nest especially difficult to find.

When the young are raised and autumn approaches, the male changes his appearance and, in some parts of the country, his name. The bright colors dim, become mottled, and he takes on more of the appearance of his dull, striped mate. In this plumage, he moves south and becomes known as the Reedbird. For generations Reedbirds have been the bane of southern rice growers, hated and hunted and a main ingredient of southern meat pies.

Each spring the Bobolink returns to its breeding grounds that extend in a wide band all across southern Canada and our northern U.S. states. Listen for the Bobolink's brilliant song in all of the Great Lakes states during the summer months.

Key Natural History References: Bent 1958, Forbush 1929, Wiens 1969.

Female

Male

Downy Woodpecker *Picoides pubescens*
Hairy Woodpecker *Picoides villosus*

The Downy Woodpecker, and its big cousin, the Hairy Woodpecker, are two year-round favorites of bird-watchers throughout the Great Lakes region. The plumage of these two birds is almost identical in color and placement, and there are only a few differences to watch for. First, the Downy is only about two-thirds the size of the Hairy, being 6 inches or thereabouts in length, while the Hairy's body is 9 inches or longer. Second, the Downy has black spots on its white tail feathers, which are lacking in the Hairy's white tail feathers. Third, and most obvious, is the difference in bill sizes. You'll note in the Downy a narrow short bill compared to the Hairy's much longer and stronger bill.

Apart from these differences, the two birds are alike in diet, habit, and range. Both are insect eaters, and they search for these by going up and down large tree trunks using short random hop-like movements, holding themselves flush against the tree, pecking at the bark, looking under bits of bark, searching for ants, beetles, flies, and any of the other high-protein insects they consume. Both are year-round residents of the entire eastern United States, and both range well beyond our borders into southern Canada. Both are fairly common at feeders throughout Michigan, both winter and summer. Both males have a red patch at the nape of their necks, and both females do not have a red patch at the nape of their necks.

When they call, you may well hear their *pik, pik* or *peek, peek* calls, both birds uttering much the same sounds as they feed. The Hairy will also "drum" with its bill against a hollow and resonant tree, while the Downy will utter a string of 10 or 15 notes in a sort of chatter. Both species nest in tree cavities, or holes drilled out of dead or living trees specially for the purpose of nesting. The Downy's entrance hole will be only about 1¼ inches in diameter; the Hairy's a full two inches. Each female lays a clutch of four or five white eggs.

The many similarities of these two species make them an attractive pair of visitors to any feeder station, and your main way of attracting them during the winter is through suet. They will cling to suet hanging in an onion sack from a hook on a porch roof, or from a tree limb, but I've had more success attaching it directly to the side of a tree, held there by onion sacking, or broken into small pieces and wedged in among the bark bumps. The birds are not particularly shy, and once they've found you, they may well stay nearby where you can watch them closely. Incidentally, both for nesting and nighttime protection, they also appreciate rough wooden boxes or sections of hollow log tucked into high-up tree crotches. Put in a sawdust floor, and you've created a wood-pecker condominium, sans mortgage!

Key Natural History References, both birds: Bent 1939, Conner et al. 1975, Graber et al. 1977, Jackson 1970, Kilham 1960, Lawrence 1967.

Downy Woodpecker   6½ inches
Hairy Woodpecker   9½ inches

Downy
Male

Downy

Females

Hairy

Eastern Phoebe *Sayornis phoebe*

Concern has been expressed in recent years over the decline in numbers of the Eastern Phoebe in the United States and special counts have been made during the last few years to determine what is happening. These flycatchers are small; they show no wing bars, or just a faint hint of them; the bill is all black; and their constant tail wagging helps you identify them. Suburban areas and ravines with low trees are the favorite habitats of the Eastern Phoebe; water must be attractive to the bird because many Phoebe nests are found on the beams and trusses of bridges.

Males of this species are not given to aerial acrobatics or fighting with other males to try to catch the attention of a female; the typical scene is for one male to follow a chosen female around, singing and calling to her. Then, when the birds pair off, the female begins to build several nests, from which she will pick and use only one. In addition to building under bridges (which happens so often that this phoebe is sometimes referred to as the "bridge" phoebe) flat places under the eaves of a house may also accommodate the nests. They are made of plant fibers, moss, and mud and are built over a period of about two weeks; the three or four eggs have fine brown dots on a dull white shell. The pairs of birds raise two broods each summer. The female sits tightly when she is incubating; it is possible to come within hand's reach of the nest before she takes flight. The male ignores the female while she is sitting, but stays in the area so he can assist in feeding the young after they emerge.

This is another bird that repeatedly parks on a tree branch and flits out quickly to snatch at airborne insects. The young learn this behavior early in life. While the adults are an undistinctive gray-brown, the young are a little more colorful than their parents; they have a light yellow breast while the adults have white breasts, gray backs, and a darker shade of gray on the head. All the flycatchers are noted for their upright stature as they sit on a branch, a point to watch for when looking for the Phoebe. This gentle little bird is light and easy on the wing, somewhat resembling a butterfly in the way it swiftly twists and turns in the air. When it alights airily on its perch, its tail keeps swaying loosely. The song of the Phoebe can be roughly interpreted as singing its own name with a downward inflection on the second syllable: *phoe-be* or *fi-bree*.

In 1840 John James Audubon attached a silver thread to the leg of a Phoebe and the first banding in history was completed. Probably it spent the winter in the southern United States or Mexico. Cowbirds intrude on this species by depositing their eggs in the Phoebe's nest; this may be one of the factors in the Phoebe's recent decline. It is a common transient and summer resident in the Lower Peninsula, uncommon in the Upper Peninsula.

Key Natural History References: Hespenheide 1971, Bent 1942, Graber et al. 1974.

White-throated Sparrow *Zonotrichia albicollis*

In the migration months of spring and fall here in our Grand Rapids latitude, we see these pretty White-throated Sparrows hopping about in thickets, or scratching for seeds on the ground beneath our feeders. Residents of the northern two-thirds of the Great Lakes region, from about the 45th Parallel northward, may see them all summer. However, the Great Lakes region is on the extreme northern edge of their winter range, so in winter we see them only infrequently. Mostly, they spend the winter in the Ohio valley and southward.

The pure white throat above the grayish breast of the adult, the bright yellow spot between the eyes, and the blackish bill are distinguishing features. Note that if the bill is *pink*, it's a White-*crowned* Sparrow, near cousin and near look-alike of the Whitethroat. The song of the White-throat has been described as sounding like *Old-Sam-Peabody-Peabody-Pea-body,* and its owner is usually seen in forest clearings, on the ground along forest edges, and along marsh borders.

The pairing-off of this bird is interesting. There's a slight color variation in head markings from bird to bird, and observers have found that those with black and white head stripes mate with birds having brown and tan head stripes. After mating, the female builds a nest on the ground or on some fallen limb hugging the ground. Typically, this will be on the edge of a clearing and well concealed. Spruce and fir forests are favored nesting locations. The nest is made of grass, twigs, wood chips, and weeds, and then lined with hair or fine rootlets.

Here the mother lays three to five, typically four, blue-white eggs with heavy markings, and then incubates them for 11 to 14 days. Her mate stays nearby singing his *Peabody* song relentlessly. The mother is a very tight nest sitter, and will not jump until an intruder is only a few feet away.

Throughout the 12 to 14 day nesting period, both parents supply the young with food, primarily weed seeds, wild fruits, and some insects. The young tend to depart from the nest before they've quite figured out how to fly, but since Whitethroats are primarily ground-dwelling birds anyway, this is not a serious problem. The adult, when fully grown, measures seven inches in body length, slightly longer than a House Sparrow.

In migration, Whitethroats fly low, do a lot of hopping along the way, and eat lots of seeds as they journey north or south, moving a bit at a time. Their journey south from our southern Michigan locale seems to take place in October, sometimes quite late in the month. I've never seen them here in large numbers, yet it's always a pleasure to see these perky members of our backyard family, whenever they arrive.

Key Natural History References: Bent 1968, Martin 1960, Fischer and Gills 1946.

Eastern Bluebird *Sialia sialis*

The bluebird means spring, and human activity stops when its sweet, musical *tru-ly* song is heard, as we quickly scan nearby trees in hopes of catching sight of this beautiful thrush. The blue on the male's back is unforgettable, combined with the rust of the breast and the white on the rump. The female has more gray on the back, and the young in their immature plumage have the streaked breasts common to the thrush family. The American Robin, for example, is another member of this family and young Robins are well known for their streaked breasts. The adult birds have a posture that seems round shouldered when they are perched.

Harsh winters can cause severe declines in the numbers of this rusty-breasted bird, however, and the efforts of the many individuals who have established "bluebird trails" in the Great Lakes region are important to their comeback. A bluebird trail is, literally, a trail of bluebird nesting houses erected along roads and in fields, usually on fence posts, in the bluebird's favorite nesting areas. Such houses, which require a round entrance hole 1½ inches in diameter, substitute for the abandoned woodpecker holes in decaying trees that were the original and natural nesting places of this bird. The 1½ inch hole is small enough to keep out Starlings, and the fence post height discourages use by Sparrows, which prefer higher locations.

Eastern Bluebirds are among the first to return North in the spring. One year, a male arrived in our yard near Grand Rapids on February 29. Such early arrival is often disastrous because of late spring storms that bring heavy, wet snow, proving rough on bluebird numbers.

But when things go well, the male stays near the chosen nest site singing his beautiful song while the female loosely arranges nesting material of grass and weeds before laying four to six pale, unmarked blue eggs. In about two weeks, the eggs hatch and both parents feed the young a diet of insects, worms, snails, berries, and fruits. The female may fly off a bit early to start another nest and, on occasion, may even pick up a new mate for her next brood. Two broods per summer are not uncommon.

Early in their life, it is possible to detect the sex of the growing birds by their emerging colors. As summer wanes, bluebirds of all ages are inclined to gather, and groups of 20 or 30 may be seen foraging together in September. Rarely do any of these birds remain with us in the cold season, even the mildest of winters. Most move to southern states for the cold months to find sufficient berries and insects.

These attractive birds can be seen in their favorite surroundings of farms, roadsides, or open country in all states east of the Great Plains. The bluebird breeds in states north of the Ohio Valley in all the Great Lakes states.

Key Natural History References: Laskey 1940, Bent 1949, Graber et al. 1971, Peakall 1970, Hartshorne 1962, Thomas 1946.

Male

Female

Cedar Waxwing *Bombycilla cedrorum*

Your first sighting of this well dressed bird will impress you with its compact, neat appearance. The Cedar Waxwing, being at seven inches just a little larger than a House Sparrow, has a fawn-colored head and back, a black mask, a saucy crest, a delicate greenish yellow on the breast, and tail feathers ending in a narrow yellow band. Be sure, as well, to note the waxy red tips on the outer wing feathers of the adult. The sexes are alike in plumage. Usually you will not see just one Cedar Waxwing, as these birds travel about in groups of 10 to 50 individuals. The only time they are inclined to be seen alone is during the nesting season in June and July. Look for this handsome bird in open woodlands, in fruiting trees and in orchards.

In nesting season, opposite sexes may pass berries to one another, in a kind of courting ritual. Watch as the male flies to a red cedar, retrieves a berry, then flies back to a waiting female and passes her the tender fruit. Berries of mountain ash, red cedar, barberry and many other small trees are the prime items of their diet. After mating, boths sexes work together in the construction of a loose nest of grass, weeds, string and twigs, with the structure typically perched at the end of a long branch. On one of our field trips, we found a nest at the end of an apple tree branch. The female sat so securely that I stroked her tail before she decided to flit away. She was warming four gray eggs splotched with brown and if all went normally, she would incubate them for just under two weeks. While she sat, her mate was nearby singing his high, thin zeeee, zeee, zeeee.

The young begin to feather out quickly and are fully feathered after two weeks in the nest, with brown streaks on the back and the breast. The young soon sit in that distinctive upright posture noted in the Waxwings, and quickly learn how to search for berries and insects. At times, these birds swoop back and forth over rivers and lakes to gather insects in the manner of a flycatcher. By fall, the babies will still not have the black mask that you see on the adults, but by the following year it will have developed.

Wherever Cedar Waxwings go they flock in large groups. I have one report from a friend who watched about 30 of them clustered together in one tree about 20 feet from the shore of Lake Michigan. In a steady, chattery stream, they flew back and forth from the tree to the water's edge, where they were bathing in the still, clear water. The total area where they splashed about, eight or ten at a time, was no bigger than a large frying pan. It looked like a communal cold tub, but they were having a merry time of it. And that was a small, late summer group. On our Christmas counts, we sometimes encounter hundreds of them. Many of the birds can be seen year-round in southern Michigan. Cedar Waxwings breed in the southern Canadian provinces and winter in an irregular, nomadic fashion from the southern half of the United States to Panama.

Key Natural History References: Putnam 1949, Bent 1950, Lea 1942.

Brown-headed Cowbird *Molothrus ater*

Mixed with the large groups of Starlings and Grackles that flock together throughout our state are sizable numbers of Brown-headed Cowbirds. All three of these birds are strongly built and aggressive, and by their sheer numbers tend to dominate activities wherever they appear. Cowbirds have an additional habit that has helped them survive, this one at the expense of many smaller, less numerous neighbors. The female Cowbird doesn't make a nest—she simply lays her eggs in the nest of any other bird she can dominate. The smaller bird then unwittingly hatches the Cowbird eggs, believing them to be her own. As the young grow, the baby Cowbird is larger, gets most of the food, and crowds out the smaller bird's young, often causing them to die of hunger. Acting as a parasite in this way, the Cowbird has been able to survive handily, at the expense of many smaller, less numerous birds. Here in Michigan, for example, Cowbirds have cut into Kirtland's Warbler populations, which are endangered. In recent times, special traps have been set up in the Kirtland's range to capture and remove Cowbirds, an approach that is believed to be working with some effectiveness.

The male Cowbird is black with a brown head, and the female is all gray; the birds hold their tails high as they stride about, walking rather than hopping. They are named Cowbirds because of their close association with grazing cattle. They are quite fearless around a herd of these animals, sometimes even riding on the cows' backs or moving about between their feet, feeding on grasshoppers and insects that cows stir up as they graze.

In spring two or three Cowbird males will be seen courting a female as they utter their whistle-like call. As noted above, however, this does not inspire her to build a nest. She usually does her laying in another bird's nest early in the morning, and may even toss out eggs of the bird she is picking on. Incubation of the Cowbird egg may not take as long as the other eggs, though this is not a certainty. It is true, however, that the baby Cowbird is usually larger than its nest mates and will monopolize the food supply coming in. Vireos, Yellow Warblers, Chipping Sparrows, and many other species are victims of the Cowbird. Cowbird chicks are gray with streaks and I have seen Indigo Buntings, Yellowthroats, and Yellow Warblers trying desperately to feed these screaming infants, which are three times as large as the poor foster mothers. There is no agreement on the number of eggs laid by the female Cowbird, but some birders have reported that it may be as high as twenty. The Cowbird is a common transient and summer resident of Michigan; it winters from southern Wisconsin and Michigan south to the Gulf Coast and Mexico.

Key Natural History References: Payne 1965, Nice 1937, Friedman 1929.

Male

Female

Hermit Thrush *Catharus guttatus*

If our list of species on a Christmas count includes a thrush, it will probably be a Hermit Thrush. Their habit of cocking their reddish-brown tail upward will help you identify them. Look for that brightly colored tail, and listen for the song that rivals the singing of the Wood Thrush. One bird watcher describes it thusly: "The song of the Hermit Thrush is a long-continued one, made up of rather long phrases of 5 to 12 notes each, with rather long pauses. All the notes are sweet, clear, and musical, like the tone of a bell, purer than the notes of a Wood Thrush, but perhaps less rich in quality. The notes in each phrase are not all connected. The first note is longest and lowest in pitch, and the final notes are likely to be grouped in twos or threes, the pitch of each group usually descending. Each phrase is similar to the others in form but on a different pitch, as if the bird sang the same theme over and over, each time in a different key." In the morning the song is likely to be cheery and spritely; in the evening, more subdued, even hymn-like. Hermits are heard less than Wood Thrushes in our area because Hermits are found mainly in the northern half of the Great Lakes region, while Wood Thrushes are found throughout our state.

Hermit Thrush nests are placed on the ground and are commonly concealed under a fern, bush, or some other overhanging vegetation. The female fashions the nest with grass, twigs, moss, and other available materials. She lays three or four eggs having a light green shell spotted with brown. While she incubates the developing embryos for 12 days, the male brings food to her; he is getting in shape for the task of feeding the young when they emerge from the eggs. As the young grow the nest is cleaned carefully and the baby birds feather out rapidly.

A pair of Hermit Thrushes will bring two or three broods into the world every summer. Because of their hurry to nest again, the parents are inclined to coax the young out of the nest before they can fly well; as a result predators may inflict heavy losses on the ground-loving thrushes. The babies that survive will look like their parents when the time for migration arrives.

Beetles are consumed in great quantities by the Hermit Thrush, and many other pesky insects are eaten by this insectivorous bird. Probably many trees in the woods where the Hermits dwell are saved from injury or destruction because they consider bark beetles such a delicacy. When these thrushes move to our southern states in winter they continue to consume many bugs; in the south Hermits are inclined to produce more singing than other members of the thrush family. When they return to us in spring, look for their nests along the northern reaches of Michigan, Minnesota, and Wisconsin, especially in jack-pine plains.

Key Natural History References: Bent 1949, Graber et al. 1971, Dilger 1956, Morse 1972.

Scarlet Tanager *Piranga olivacea*

Many people have asked me, "What is the prettiest bird that visits your yard?" "The male Scarlet Tanager," is always my immediate reply. No bird book can adequately portray this gorgeous red male with his black wings when he parks on the stump by my birdbath.

Scarlet Tanagers are between the size of a Sparrow and a Robin, with the male a bright red and the female yellow-green with black to gray wings. She seems to take a back seat to her brilliant mate, at least in terms of color. He sings like a hoarse Robin—*chip-burr, chip-burr*—a typical song being four or five short phrases. While he sings she builds a crude nest some distance out on the limb of an oak or maple; the nest may be 30 to 50 feet high in the tree. Building materials include twigs, grass, rootlets, and finer strands of the same materials for the lining. She lays usually four pale blue-green eggs that are lightly spotted with brown, and incubates them by herself for about two weeks.

The babies fly from the nest looking quite a bit like their mother. As fall approaches the scarlet male begins to molt and becomes an amazing sight; his colors now include red, yellow, and green, and seeing these molting males has always been an arresting sight for me. He wears the drab coat of the adult female all winter and then his radiant red attire returns for the springtime trip to the nesting country around us. Young males may take two years to attain the full splendor of the older males.

After both parents have fed the young for a time, the whole family concentrates on an insect diet that helps control our bug populations. In the fall the family departs for Central and South America.

Scarlet Tanagers are not spritely, lively birds. Their movements are often slow, almost lethargic. They are not prone to display their colors and that's why they are not often seen, even though they possess brilliant, conspicuous plumage. Their song is often mistaken for that of a Robin, or even that of a Rose-breasted Grosbeak or a Red-eyed Vireo, so it is difficult to locate them by their song. When these fascinating birds return to Michigan in spring almost everyone will take a second look if that flash of red comes into view. You will want to tell all your friends about the attractive male when you have your first encounter with him. They are a common summer resident in deciduous woods throughout most of the state, although uncommon to scarce in the northern Upper Peninsula and on Isle Royale.

Key Natural History References: Prescott 1965, Bent 1958.

Female

Male

"Baltimore" or Northern Oriole

Icterus galbula

Our birdbaths are a favorite spot for these colorful birds from April or May through September. The shiny flame-orange and black males with their solid black heads are a bit smaller than a Robin—about seven and one-half inches long. The spectacular coloring of the male will catch your attention. The female is a duller burnt orange-yellow and olive-brown—not as brilliantly colored as the male but equally attractive. Although the official name for this bird is the Northern Oriole, many bird watchers will always think of these fascinating and colorful creatures as the "Baltimore" Orioles.

Soon after the arrival of the Orioles during the first days of May, I unravel strands of binder twine and drape them in our backyard trees. Why? Because the female Oriole loves to swing back and forth pulling on the twine as she attempts to get a mouthful of this valuable nesting material. She will spend five or six days weaving her nest in an oak, maple, willow, or some other deciduous tree. The opening of the pendulous, hanging nest usually is near the top where the strands are woven over the top of the supporting tree limb. Construction materials include string, hair, plant fibers and other tough material, and the nest generally is a slate gray color. It is fairly common for these Orioles to build in the same tree as other species; they seem to relate well to their neighbors.

The Northern Oriole's eggs, about five in number, are grayish-blue to white with obvious scrawls and streaks of black or dark brown. The female incubates them for 12 to 14 days, raises just one brood per summer, and tends to her family for about two weeks before they are able fly away. The young are the burnt orange color of their mother. The young sometimes creep about on the outside of the nest when they are only a week old. The male and female both protect the nest vigorously, and I've seen Blue Jays suffer the wrath of angry Orioles. The Oriole has a rich piping whistled song, and the young often plead *tee-deedee* when begging for insects or any fruit brought to the nest.

There is evidence that Baltimore Orioles return year after year to the same nesting location, and possibly even to the same tree where they were hatched. If so, what a remarkable navigator this little bird is, flying back and forth between North and South America and making such accurate landings in the process.

With Baltimore in its name, it's not surprising that this is the state bird of Maryland. In October, these birds leave us to visit their winter homes in Central and South America. But it's always a bright spring day, no matter what the weather, when these radiant orange and black birds return to us. They love the open woods found in our Great Lakes region, but they range over a wide area, and breed from Wyoming, Alberta, and Nova Scotia, to Texas and Georgia. They can be spotted throughout the Great Lakes region during summer months.

Key Natural History References: Bent 1958, Forbush 1929.

Female

Male

Horned Lark *Eremophila alpestris*

Wide open spaces are the habitat of this species; airports and golf courses and cutover grain fields are especially choice places for them. Several times I have found nests of this lark in the middle of a fairway, the eggs hardly visible from a distance of six feet. If you have a lawn that's open and wide, you may attract some of these ground-loving birds as well. Some Horned Larks stay with us all winter and group together in fields; they especially appreciate fields where the farmer has a policy of spreading manure fresh from the barn. Horned Larks and other species such as Snow Buntings and Longspurs will frequently follow the farmer's manure spreader as it tosses the organic substance over a large area. Horned Larks are a little larger than House Sparrows and have a black line running from each side of the bill and turning down; another single black patch runs across the upper chest. Tiny dark colored "horns" which are really just feathers are present on top of the head but are not always easily seen. Horned Lark backs are streaked brown, their tail is brown, and their breast off-white. These larks nest early, so late snowstorms are a continuing seasonal problem. Courtship includes some very high flights that occur in February and March. The nest is a simple depression in the ground; the female prepares it in just a couple of days. Being such an early nester, it is not unusual to see this bird sitting on a nest completely surrounded by snow. More commonly, they are surrounded by dried grasses in late winter and use these for camouflage.

Eggs are gray-green with peppery spotting and are difficult to see, when the camouflaged batch of four lies in the uncovered nest on the ground. Babies sit tight and close in the nest, but will wander away from it to forage at an early age; the mother flies from the nest when intruders are some distance away, so the site is hard to detect. Two broods are raised each summer. The two calls of the Horned Lark are not really songs. In the winter, when alarmed and flying off, they utter a one, two, or three part high-pitched call. Their spring nesting "song" is a rapid series of one or two phrases that vary in length and pitch, but which are generally weak.

Some winters we have many Horned Larks staying with us. If you are out skiing, or during a drive, watch for them along country roads as they congregate on plowed fields. Horned Larks are gregarious, and it's not uncommon to find them in sizeable flocks during cold months. In summer, however, you will be more likely to get them singly or in pairs. Seeds and grains are the prime diet items of Horned Larks in the winter, but they supplement this with field insects in the warm months.

Key Natural History References:
Pickwell, Sutton 1927, Bent 1942.

98

Rose-breasted Grosbeak

Pheucticus ludovicianus

What a spring tonic it is to see the arrival of these elegant red, black, and white birds in our yard early in May. They arrive in spring on such a regular schedule we can almost predict the exact day. Rose-breasted Grosbeaks are a bit smaller than a Robin, with a solid, strong-looking body structure. The brilliant bib of the male will help you make an instant identification. The female on the other hand looks like a very large sparrow with a light line over her eye. The very large blunt bill of both sexes, similar to a Cardinal's, assures you that these are seed-eating birds.

Both male and female grosbeaks sing lustily during courtship, and the males sometimes engage in pitched battles to win a mate. When pairing has been established, both prospective parents work to build a nest about 15 feet high in a deciduous tree. If you judge their work by the type of nest that results you will say they are poor workers; the nest is made of twigs and it is often possible to see the blue sky as you look up through the nest from below. As the male flies away, displaying his beautiful black and white pattern, it is interesting to note that such a pretty bird is such an indifferent nest builder.

The eggs average about four in number and are blue to green with brown spots; the spots are concentrated on the large end of the egg. Incubation of the eggs lasts approximately 14 days, and when the nestlings leave for their first flight it is easy to tell whether they are males or females; the males have pink or red on the underside of the wing, while the females have a lining of feathers that is a delicate orange-yellow color. The adult female could be confused with the female Purple Finch (see page 60), but this Grosbeak is much larger. adult female.

The song of the Rose-breasted Grosbeak is very similar to a Robin's, though mellower—a series of rapid notes connected for the most part by liquid consonant sounds. Some describe the song as a warble, although there are definite, short pauses in the singing. Rarely are two successive notes on the same pitch. The male often sings while on the nest; the female's song is softer and shorter than the male's.

These attractive birds have been increasing in numbers in our area. They are a common transient and summer resident throughout Michigan—with the exception of Isle Royale, where they are less frequently found. They will stay with us until early October before departing for Central or South America. They help make our summer days brighter as they search about for seeds and insects in the leafy trees of Michigan.

Key Natural History References: Bent 1968, Gabrielson 1915.

Male

Female

Rufous-sided Towhee *Pipilo erythrophthalmus*

Leaves and debris on the forest floor fly in every direction when Towhees decide to scratch for food. If you can get close enough at such a time, you'll see how much they look like tiny barnyard chickens, scratching and pecking, scratching and pecking. Their principal foods are insects, seeds, fruits, and mast. Towhees are a bit smaller than Robins, though not as chunky in body structure. The male Towhee has a black head, bib, and back, with brick red to chestnut colored sides and a pure white breast. The female has all the same colors in the same pattern, but her head, bib, and back are a rich, deep brown instead of black. Together, they're a very colorful pair.

They spend most of their time on or near the ground. Their nests are a loose cup built either on the ground or only a few feet up, usually in a low, dense bush. Only in the nesting season, when the female is snugly settled in her low nest, will the male go to a higher perch to sing and call and so signify the territory he controls. His song sounds like a happy *drink your tea, drink your tea,* repeated many times each minute. He also sings *towhee, towhee,* a habit which gave him his name in the first place. Meantime, the female warms the eggs on their nest of grass, weed stalks, and twigs. Many Towhee nests are lined with animal hair, gathered where former owners left it on thorns and bristly bushes, which gives the nest a warm, soft appearance. Working alone, the female builds this structure in about five days, then deposits three to six, but typically three or four eggs and settles down to wait developments.

The eggs are white or gray with light brown spots. Twice each summer she lays such a batch and each time raises her broods to flight age, a schedule which leaves her little time for anything else. The birds are rather secretive in nature, but it's believed that the same pair remains mated through each year for at least two, and perhaps on occasion even a third brood.

The young, when they feather out and begin to move about, are marked with streaks on the back and sides, and do not have the red eye of the adults. Mostly you'll see these youngsters in the fall, shortly before migration. Incidentally, the white markings on the Towhee's tail are not too easily seen when the birds are walking about or scratching for food. However, they have a tail flicking habit that exposes those white tail patches to view.

Occasionally a hardy, lost, or perhaps foolish Towhee will stay with us all winter. Usually, however, we see them here in the lakes states only during the warm months because all but a few travel to the southern states and Mexico well ahead of snowfall.

One thing about these birds: When you meet them, you'll know and remember them. Their bright colors, songs, and habits are distinctive and unforgettable.

Key Natural History References: Bent 1968, Davis 1960.

Male

Female

Red-winged Blackbird *Agelaius phoeniceus*

Of all our many regional blackbirds the Redwing is the one that's most attractive to me. The male arrives early in spring and his cheerful, gurgling *o-ka-lee* or *konk-lar-ree* is one of the first bird sounds of the year we hear. The jet black body plumage of the males, offset by the bright red shoulder marks and wing chevrons of yellow, show this bird at his best in his spring uniform. Females are brown with heavy stripes running along their breasts. Redwings are almost Robin size, ranging between seven and nine and one-half inches long.

It is the male that arrives first in the Great Lakes region, returning to his northern breeding grounds here in southern Michigan in early March, and a bit later in the Upper Peninsula. His first task is to find a suitable marshy habitat where he can establish a territory. There he perches on cattails, or in the still leafless trees of late winter to sing lustily and fly at all intruders who near the borders of his chosen territory. The female's arrival and the mating and nest building begin a week or two later.

The nest, built by the female, is usually in reeds near or above water. It is built of sedge, grass, and rushes, and is a bulky, well camouflaged affair which occasionally ties together a few stems from nearby cattails. She warms her three to six speckled eggs for nearly two weeks while her mate patrols the nest area. The male is a courageous, almost fearless defender of the nest. He will swoop down from a treetop, coming closer and closer until, at times, he will strike a person on the head in dive-bomb fashion. At other times, when undisturbed, he sings loudly and melodiously from a vantage point near the nest. Both parents feed the young a diet rich in protein, mainly from insects, but also with some weed seeds.

In mid-August, Redwings congregate in company with Cowbirds, Grackles, Blackbirds, and Starlings, and sometimes cause substantial damage to the grainfields they frequent. They become part of those great rolling masses of birds seen in our sky each fall. By mid-October, they fly in these great flocks to the Ohio Valley and beyond, where they often prove a winter problem to residents of the States of Kentucky, Tennessee and Maryland. Most of these assertive, gregarious birds live year-round in states south of the Great Lakes and east of the Rockies. But each spring, large numbers also migrate to breeding grounds throughout the Great Lakes region. Watch for this colorful bird during the winter months in southern Minnesota, Wisconsin and southwestern Michigan.

Key Natural History References: Bent 1958, Orians 1961, Case and Hewitt 1963.

Male

Female

Purple Martin *Progne subis*

If you are lucky enough to have Purple Martins in your vicinity, you will probably see a lot of them as they are gregarious, and colony roosting types. However, there are major gaps in the distribution of this bird, and many places that should prove ideal to Purple Martins seem unable to attract them. This is a puzzling situation that has yet to be understood by anyone but the Purple Martin.

Purple Martins like open agricultural country, or grassy semi-open areas and, if regionally present, they will readily nest in boxes or colony houses placed on poles in the open. The poles should be 15 to 20 feet high, the size of each compartment 6 by 6 by 6 inches and the hole opening 2½ inches in diameter, placed an inch above the box floor.

The adult males are quite dark, and appear black against a light sky; however, there is a purplish-black iridescence on both their backs and stomach areas which can be seen in the right conditions. The females and young of both sexes are light-colored on their breasts, and are probably most easily distinguished from other swallows by their association with the adult males, as there is no other swallow having a dark belly. The flight of the Purple Martin is an alternation of flaps and sails, and typically they fly in circles, snapping down insects in flight.

Purple Martins are summer residents in the Great Lakes region. The male scouts arrive here in early April to search for nesting and roosting sites. Long ago, Indians hung groups of gourds on trees to create primitive apartment complexes for the Martins; today our more elaborate apartment buildings also please these birds. When the females arrive a little later in April they choose a good apartment and a desirable male.

Nests are built by both birds of grasses, leaves, trash, and pieces of paper; five pure white eggs are laid in this nest, and the female does all the sitting while her mate hovers close by catching insects and singing on the wing *chew, chew, peew, peew.* She sits for two weeks, and then the babies are fed by both parents. The menu is almost exclusively made up of insects. Your summer evenings will be filled with the incessant gurgling of these birds if they occupy a Martin apartment house nearby and you provide them a source of drinking water.

The tremendous aggregations of Swallows and Martins has caused difficulty in some towns along the migration route. However, the birds will stay only a brief time in any one place before they wing their way to Central and South America, and certainly their value as insect eaters outweighs the brief problem caused by the huge flocks stopping for a rest on their way to a winter abode.

Key Natural History References:
Finlay 1971, Allen and Nice 1952,
Bent 1942.

Male

Female

European Starling *Sturnus vulgaris*

In fall and winter streams of Starlings may be seen flowing into a grove of trees for as long as half an hour in some areas of Kentucky, Tennessee, and other states. The seeds for this fantastic Starling crop were sown in 1890, when a few of these birds were released in Central Park in New York to enjoy the freedom of America. They were imported from England by a misguided bird-lover who thought they'd be a nice addition to our wildlife scene. For the first six years, they were found only within the greater New York City limits. By 1900 they had spread to New Jersey and Connecticut; Massachusetts didn't see its first Starling until 1908. By 1926, all of New England, Pennsylvania, Virginia, and most of the Ohio River Valley were included in the Starling's range. Today they can be found year-round in every state in the continental U.S., and in southern Canada during the summer. Because of their great numbers, their unclean nests, their habit of molesting other birds, and the damage they do to farmer's crops, Starlings are regarded as a "nuisance" bird.

Starlings have black to brown feathers and a yellow bill in summer which darkens in winter. Their strongly-built body ends in a short, blunt tail. They nest anywhere and toss out many desirable species from any nest site they want. Unkempt nests of grass, leaves, and feathers are thrown together in nest boxes, under eaves, in natural holes in trees, and in any secure cavity, and are often placed near the nests of other birds. Their eggs, four or five in number, are generally pale blue or green. Males help the females in incubation for two weeks, and then help feed the chicks for up to three weeks in the nest.

Except when roosting as a colony, Starlings are not inclined to inhabit thick forests and the only time they invade my forested yard is in winter when they hunger for suet. If your feeders are located in more open ground you may expect them to visit. Also look for these gregarious birds to descend in noisy droves on any cutover grain field or some open, grassy area. They flock with Redwings, Grackles, and Cowbirds. Starlings are wary so it's easy to scare them away to your neighbor's field—in case you don't like your neighbor.

When a dense stand of trees is chosen for a roosting site you can hear the squeaking, chattering mob all night long as they jostle one another. Early in the morning they will fly in mass formation to nearby fields where food is available. In fall and winter the adults will have many more light spots on their feathers and the gray feathered young will be numerous in every flock. Some will stay with us all winter, but most will leave to pester the citizens of the Ohio and Mississippi River valleys. Christmas counts in Arkansas and Missouri often include millions of these brown, speckled creatures.

Key Natural History References: Kessel 1957, Dunnett 1955, Williamson and Gray 1975.

Winter

Summer

Northern Cardinal *Cardinalis cardinalis*

The rich red of the male cardinal is seen at our feeders most often in the early morning hours and during the hour just before sunset though they willingly change this habit when ample supplies of sunflower and other seeds are provided at feeders. Females, who are a bit more timid than the males, are tawny brown with a rusty red showing through here and there. In short, both are beautifully colored, although quite different. The sexes will appear in mixed groups in winter, sometimes in clusters of 20 to 30 at a time. However, a good signal that spring is here is to see a male take a seed in his beak, hop across a short distance, lean forward, and offer it delicately to a receptive female. All year, each bird seems to have a specific mate, but paying such special attention to one another appears to occur only when it is time to build a nest.

The orange-red bill of both sexes is blunt and strong and surrounded by a line of hair-like black feathers. The uplifted crest on their heads gives these birds a very classy and sassy appearance. Northern Cardinals are not particularly friendly, and will normally remain at a respectable distance from the human species. I've banded a great many, but they have to be held with gloves to prevent deep peck wounds. Early in the spring, both sexes will notify you of their presence with any of several songs. The sharp, one syllable whistle is the most noticeable, but if possible watch for these birds and learn to identify their varied calls. How many calls do they have? Three or four at least, ranging from *what-cheer-cheer-cheer*, to *birdy-birdy-*

birdy-birdy, to the single note whistle.

Most Northern Cardinals build their nests less than 10 feet above the ground in bushes, thickets, conifers and brushy areas. The loosely built nests consist of twigs, weeds, grass, bark and leaves and are often lined with animal hair and feathers. The female lays three or four white to blue-green eggs that are spotted and streaked with smears of red-brown to lavender, mainly on the blunt end of the egg, which will hatch about 13 days after incubation begins. The female normally does most of the sitting, with the male bringing food to her during this period. Both parents work together to feed the young a diet of seeds after hatching.

The Northern Cardinal stays in the Great Lakes region all winter and nests here as well. The birds can be found in all states east of the Rockies, although in Michigan, Minnesota, and Wisconsin they generally stay in the southern part of the state. You'll frequently see them flying low across the road ahead of your car just as Brown Thrashers often do. In winter, we're always thrilled by the sight of a group of these brilliantly colored birds hopping about on bushes, or flocking across our yard, especially during the white months of January and February. It is not surprising that so many states claim this colorful creature as their state bird.

Key Natural History References: Lasky 1944, Dow 1969, Bent 1968.

110

Northern Cardinal   7½-9 inches

Female

Male

Eastern Kingbird *Tyrannus tyrannus*

Eastern Kingbirds are common, conspicuous, and easy to identify. They are between a Robin and a Sparrow in size, and the white band across the ends of the tail feathers is an obvious key to recognition. Kingbirds have a habit of sitting on open branches or fence wires and suddenly flashing out after a flying insect, then returning to their perch. Insects comprise about 90 percent of their diet.

These birds are fearless and defiant, and unlike most birds, whose concern is usually restricted to the immediate vicinity of their nests, Kingbirds will sit on a perch commanding a clear view of the surrounding countryside and will drive off any bird they think is invading their territory. Kingbirds seem to regard any big bird as an enemy; whenever a crow, vulture, hawk, or any other sizeable bird appears nearby, the Kingbird will usually dash off and give chase, flying around and pecking at it till it leaves. Size seems to make no difference; pilots of small airplanes should take note.

In mating season these birds have been seen somersaulting in the air as they try to impress a prospective mate. After pairing is completed, both sexes work together to build an unkempt nest of weeds and grass on the limb of a tree; the nests are usually about 15 feet above the ground and often are near water. Old orchards frequently have a few pairs of Kingbirds in residence; the three to five eggs that are laid are creamy white with dark spots of brown, black, and purple. Some birders say that the eggs of the Kingbird are the most colorful of any species that nest in our area.

Kingbirds are poor singers, so defense of their rather small territory is primarily done by chasing intruders they don't like. The eggs hatch after the female incubates them for 12 or 13 days, and the babies grow for two weeks in the nest before they leave home.

Watch for the Eastern Kingbird in every type of open habitat. The classy black and white of the bird and the white edging of the tail feathers is unmistakable. Also, it's erect upright posture is characteristic. In fall the birds migrate during the day to South America, where they find an abundance of the insects on which to feed till our cold months have passed and they can return here once again.

Key Natural History References: Bent 1942, Graber et al. 1974, Johnston 1971.

112

Evening Grosbeak *Hesperiphona vespertina*

You may not be able to add this bird to your list this year—or any year soon, but be patient. The Evening Grosbeak, a gregarious bird a bit smaller than a Robin, visits us according to a very erratic schedule. It is a common summer resident in the Upper Peninsula, but those of us in the southern part of Michigan only see them during winter months. Growing to a length of eight inches, the male is a real color spectacle—a yellow body with black crown and tail, and black and white wings. The female and young have yellow napes and sides, no yellow over the eye, and smoky gray bodies. If large groups journey your way, be sure you are well-stocked with sunflower seeds—they consume great quantities each day. Some bird watchers have dubbed this species "grocery beaks" for the quantity of food they eat. Their boldness and numbers very likely will keep other birds away, but they are definitely worth the temporary disruption and you will enjoy them every minute.

This grosbeak was given the common name of "evening" because the first ornithologist who described it believed it sang its short, uneven, *chirp-cleer* or *clee-ip* only towards sunset, when it stirred from its dwelling at the approach of night. But this idea has since been disproven, and you may hear it sing at all times of the day. These birds are especially vocal during mating season when they dance about excitedly. We normally don't see this courtship display, however; it most often occurs in Canada in the conifer and maple woods the grosbeak calls home.

The female builds a shallow nest of twigs high in a large evergreen. Most nests are about 40 feet above the ground, of loose and indifferent construction. Twice each summer she lays two to five, typically three or four, blue to blue-green eggs that are streaked with brown, gray, or black. Then she nestles down snugly for the incubation period, the male bringing her all of her meals. She sits for 12 to 13 days, seldom leaving the nest for more than a few minutes.

Both parents feed the young regurgitated food for the first few days. Nesting among evergreens provides them with an ample food supply of spruce budworms. It is interesting to note that in maturity these same birds will shift to a diet consisting of 95 percent vegetable matter. They often crunch seeds and fruit pits that can be opened only with that powerful beak—a large, blunt, conical bill that is gray-ivory in winter and pale green in spring. But buds and soft maple seeds are their mainstays.

Each winter we look for the arrival of the Evening Grosbeak, although it often disappoints us. Think snow! Scarcely ever does one make an appearance during our mild, open winters. Besides occasional treks into Michigan, this once strictly western resident now roams as far east as Massachusetts and south to the Carolinas. Its normal year-round range, however, is along the Canadian border.

Key Natural History References: Bent 1968, Belknap 1973, Parks 1963.

114

Male

Female

Wood Thrush *Hylocichla mustelina*

Throughout the dense woodlands of the Great Lakes states, the handsome Wood Thrush nests and forages for food on the forest floor. The Wood Thrush, Hermit Thrush, Veery, Swainson's Thrush, and Gray-cheeked Thrush will all be seen at one time or another in this habitat, but they may also become part of your backyard community if you have tall trees or dense forest nearby.

The best way to recognize and separate these species, one from the other, is to note what portion of their heads and backs is covered with reddish-brown rather than drab gray-brown. Only the Wood Thrush's crown is cinnamon-brown in color; other thrushes which look similar have red-brown tails, but their heads are a drab gray-brown. These are not major differences, and even when seen together, it's not always easy to sort out this little group of forest dwellers.

The *call* of the Wood Thrush is a series of quick notes *tick, tick, tick* or *pit, pit,* uttered in rapid succession. By contrast, the *song* is flutelike and runs on and on in groups of three to five notes, broken by brief pauses. Sometimes low notes and sometimes trills are included. These are sweet sounds, sung only by the male which signals all nearby that the Wood Thrush is present and will defend its nest with vigor.

The nest of this thrush, placed in a site chosen by the female, is built of grass, weeds, paper, mud, and leaf mold, all hardened into a neat cup. Usually, the nest is placed either on the ground or not more than a few feet above ground. There the female lays an average of four blue-green eggs and nesting begins. The female incubates these eggs for two weeks, nestling them close under her breast against her "brood spot," an area of bare skin seen on many species during the nesting season.

After hatching, the young are fed a diet of insects that have been gathered by both parents during foraging efforts along the forest floor. They eat small wild fruits as well, so your feeder should include raisins, bits of apple, and other small chunks of fruit. Essentially, the Wood Thrush is a bird of the forest floor that has adapted to humans invading its native habitat, so if you do not have ample quantities of tall shade trees nearby, this bird may not appear at your feeders. On the other hand, where humans, tall trees, and moist bottomlands are found together, the Wood Thrush is likely to appear, and when it searches for food on your lawn, you'll note its habits are similar to those of the Robin, another member of the Thrush family.

Wood Thrushes summer throughout the Great Lakes region, but by mid-October they are on the wing to Central America, their winter home. That's a long flight for a little bird, but in the spring they'll return once again and bring us their handsome brown selves and their flutelike songs.

Key Natural History References:
Graber et al. 1971, Bent 1949, Dilger 1956, Bertin 1977, Longcore 1969.

Great Crested Flycatcher *Myiarchus crinitus*

The yellow belly, gray throat, rufous tail, and rather large bill are striking features of Great Crested Flycatchers. Their length is just a little less than a Robin; their song is a distinctive series of ascending notes, a loud whistled *wheep!* or a rolling *prrrrrreet!* If you get close enough these birds look as though they sport a crew cut, and their habit of launching into the air suddenly from an open perch, and then returning to it, tell you they are one of the flycatcher family.

In addition to these short sallies in chase of flies and other insects, the Great Crested has three other distinct flight patterns: First, its hovering flight on rapidly beating wings is similar to the Eastern Kingbird's; second, when hunting insects it flies swiftly after its prey in erratic dashes, in typical flycatcher fashion; and third, when not hunting it often sails from one tree to another on motionless wings, in a gliding fashion similar to that used by the Blue Jay.

Nests are unusual structures built in old woodpecker holes or natural cavities in trees; the birds will readily accept a hollowed out log that you have mounted on a post. Junk and trash of all kinds, plus snakeskins, frequently are added to the nest; both the parents bring in a supply of material to build it for a period of two weeks. The off-white eggs, usually five in number, are heavily spotted with dark colors that cover almost the whole shell and are laid in a small cup that is formed in the maze of materials.

Females incubate for two weeks, and the young stay in the nest for two weeks after hatching. Males help feed the young on insect larvae, so our trees benefit from the food gathering habits of these flycatchers. It is true that the nests are constructed of all types of trash, but the parents are careful to remove all excretory material from it; sanitation by this bird is meticulous.

In the past some birders hypothesized that the snakeskins which are so often present in the Great Crested's nest were placed there to discourage predators; this has been discounted however, as the bird seems to gather the skins as it would just another piece of trash. A few other species include snakeskins in their nests—it seems that this is simply a collector's item for several birds. Great Crested Flycatchers are common in the Lower Peninsula, uncommon in the Upper. They leave us in September or October to winter in Mexico and Central America where they find an abundant supply of insects, the major part of their diet.

Key Natural History References: Graber et al. 1974, Bent 1942, Allen 1933a, Mousley 1934.

Yellow-bellied Sapsucker

Sphyrapicus varius

The name of this member of the woodpecker family is very appropriate for both its color and behavior. The males sport yellow bellies, black bodies, long white wing patches, and red throat and forehead patches. The female is much the same color, though she has no red on her head, substituting instead a white throat patch. If you find a tree (or even sometimes the wall of an old wooden building) with a series of shallow, pencil-diameter holes in a spiral or horizontal pattern, a Sapsucker has been at work. These holes are made by the birds to produce and catch a supply of flowing sap, and some trees are seriously damaged, or killed, if the excavations become too numerous. The Sapsucker returns periodically to check the holes and to suck up the sugar-rich sap that flows into them.

These birds are only a tad shorter than a Robin, having a body about eight inches long. In spring, early May through June, the pair picks a tree with rotten heartwood for the nest, usually a tree not less than 10 inches in trunk diameter and preferably an aspen or birch. There they hollow out a cavity in the trunk anywhere from 8 to 40 feet above the ground. The nest inside the hole is often more than a foot deep and has a floor of wood chips on which the eggs are laid. The clutch may vary from two to seven eggs, but typically has five or six, all pure white. Both sexes spend time incubating the eggs over a period of 12 to 14 days, after which the hatched young remain in the nest another 24 to 26 days before attempting flight. Very early in their lives the young are treated to meals of sap, carried to the nest in the throat of the adults. They also are fed the soft inner bark of trees and small insects, as well as small fruits and berries, and these foods—half animal and half vegetable—become their principal diet in adult life.

Sapsuckers are moderately common in the northern Great Lakes region, but easily overlooked by backyard watchers, as they prefer mixed hardwood-conifer forests, small clearings near water, and orchards. Still, if you live in areas of this region where aspens and birches are common, you may easily see these birds from your kitchen window. You may also see them in the southern Great Lakes region during migration, as they travel south to Central America, Mexico, and our southern states in the fall. They return north in the spring to the aspen-birch forests typical of the northern Great Lakes region. It is fun to have some of these attractive agile birds around your yard, but that may dim as you note the damage done to healthy trees being tapped for sap. Still, plenty of insects also are eaten by Sapsuckers, so perhaps that balances their tree drilling.

Key Natural History References: Lawrence 1967, Howell 1952, Graber et al. 1977, Bent 1939, Kilham 1962.

Pine Grosbeak *Pinicola enucleator*

The Pine Grosbeak is an occasional winter visitor to Michigan, when for some reason numbers of them appear throughout the Great Lakes region. On such occasions, young birds seem to outnumber the adults. Together, they'll be seen in the winter countryside, along streets, and at feeding stations throughout Michigan.

The Pine Grosbeak is a quiet, robin-sized bird with a short, powerful rounded bill, a medium length notched tail and white wing bars. It is most often confused with the Purple Finch, but the finch is a sparrow-sized bird and has a small bill and dull wing bars. The White-winged Crossbill, which is similar, also is smaller and has a crossed bill.

The female Pine Grosbeak is similar to the Evening Grosbeak except that it is less stocky and has a longer tail, while the Evening Grosbeak sports large white wing patches rather than bars.

The immature Pine Grosbeak male looks like the female but has a red wash on its head and rump. Its color tint is as often dull yellow as pink. In poor winter light this plump bird appears to be dull gray.

Pine Grosbeaks prefer the edges of conifer forests where they are often seen feeding on mountain ash and sumac berries. This bird is remarkably easy to approach, having so little fear of humans as to appear stupid in its behavior. It generally is seen in flocks and spends much of its time sitting still or moving about so slowly it seems totally engrossed in its feeding and oblivious to all that goes on around it. Its flight is marked by a decided un-dulation, rising and falling in a looping pattern that is distinctive.

This grosbeak's call is a clear whistled *you, you, you* and loud musical warbles in a three-syllabled *tee, tee, tew*. In fact, it's often a beautiful melody of several sounds, some loud and some soft, and a real treat to hear. Unlike many birds, the Pine Grosbeak sings in flight, as well as when perched.

Winter food in Michigan includes the buds of pine, spruce and tamarack trees. It especially seeks maple seeds and in Canada, where it spends its summers, it is fond of berries. If Pine Grosbeaks come to your feeder some winter soon you might be treated to a lengthy visit, so put out bits of apple, raisins, and other fruits along with pine nuts, and perhaps this handsome bird will remain with you for several days.

In spring this favorite, although infrequent visitor to Michigan returns to its nesting grounds in the forests of Canada. If you travel to Ontario, you'll almost certainly see this bird in pine and spruce forests around the north shore of Lake Superior.

Key Natural History References: Bent 1968, Harrison 1975.

Male

Female

Red-headed Woodpecker

Melanerpes erythrocephalus

Some areas of the United States have reported declining populations of this handsome woodpecker, and if true that would be tragic. The head is a solid red color and the body is black and white; it is the only woodpecker with a completely red head. When the bird takes flight the large, square white patches on its wings stand out boldly. Their feet are equipped with very sharp, large claws. As a registered bird-bander, I have held many woodpeckers and the Redheads definitely have the most strength of any I've ever held.

A stand of dead trees such as you find in a backwater area or a dead elm in your back yard are places to watch the Redheads. They are inclined to live in open woods and on the edges of thick forests. If there is a lack of trees, these birds may choose a telephone pole or a sturdy wooden post for their home. They relish oak trees, but probably only for the acorns they provide, as up to half the diet of this bird is vegetable matter, including berries, acorns, and apples.

After a pair has excavated a hole about 16 inches deep in a soft tree, the female lays her four or five white eggs. Both parents take turns incubating the clutch. Two weeks after hatching, the young flutter out on their own. The heads of the young are grayish-brown and the distinct black and white pattern is absent for many weeks. It will be late fall before they have any red on them. Two broods may be raised each summer. Listen for their flicker-like call of *kik-kik-kik* as they learn to communicate.

Large sharply-pointed bills are used by Redheads to capture insects in flight, but their diet is so dependent on vegetable matter that a missed insect here or there hardly matters. The birds use their powerful flight and aggressiveness to defend their home territory in breeding season. These woodpeckers sometimes prove very tough toward other bird species. They will attack smaller birds, driving them from their nests, robbing them of their eggs or young; they will fight other birds, such as Starlings and smaller woodpeckers, for a coveted nesting hole. They are jealous of their food supply and will drive other birds away from their favorite feeding places. But toward other Redheads they are often indifferent or accepting, contrary to the habits of most territorial birds.

Red-headed Woodpeckers can be found year-round from the Great Plains east, including southern Minnesota, Wisconsin, and Michigan; they breed in the northern Great Lakes and Great Plains area. Seldom do we see them at our suet feeders, but when I scatter cracked corn on the ground after the snow is gone Redheads drop around every day for a snack.

Key Natural History References: Conner 1976, Reller 1972, Graber et al. 1977, Bent 1939.

Gray Catbird *Dumetella carolinensis*

Catbirds are about the length of a Robin but have a sleek, streamlined build compared to the stout, heavy Robin's body. Nearly all their feathers are gray except for a black cap and some rufous coverts under the tail. You will see them flying just above the ground. I cannot recall ever seeing a Catbird perched more than 15 feet above ground in a tree.

Early in the morning Gray Catbirds carry on a constant chatter. Apparently they try to imitate other birds, but they usually do a poor job, their mimics coming out as a mix of various calls. They are secretive and are ready to sound like an angry cat if you disturb their nests, usually located a few feet above ground level in a bush. Often the nest will be placed close to a marshy area, constructed of twigs, grass, and rootlets. No matter where they are found, nests are always well concealed. Both members of a pair work on the nest and make a rather deep container for the eggs.

The song of the Catbird comes to us early in May when the birds arrive from Central America and our southern states. After mating and nest building are completed, the female will be ready to sit on four unmarked greenish-blue eggs. The male moves about the nest area with his tail cocked high, singing for many hours of the day. Both parents bring food to the young and this species is famous for keeping the nest very tidy.

It's interesting to note that someone took time to count the feathers of one Catbird and the total numbered 1733. The weight of these feathers, however, constituted only one-fifteenth of the total weight of the bird. This ratio is true of most species and gives us some idea of the lightness of a bird's body covering.

Catbirds eat more vegetable matter than animal material. They consume lots of wild fruit, and also eat many insects that might damage fruit-bearing trees and bushes. Their habit of remaining near ground level at all times makes them vulnerable to predators such as cats, snakes, and foxes. Cowbirds have not been much of a detriment to the Catbird because this gray bird has somehow learned to toss strange eggs out of its nest.

Gray Catbirds present a very neat appearance. They are quick and friendly with a lively, playful temperment. They will rush to the aid of other Catbirds who are in trouble; many times you see another Catbird coming to the aid of parents defending their nest or young, all adults working together to present a raucous noisy front. Look for this bird during the summer, although they will occasionally spend the winter here in sparse numbers. They are found mainly in shrubby habitats. Most members of this species spend the winter in the deep south, mainly in Florida and around the Gulf of Mexico.

Key Natural History References: Nickell 1965, Graber et al. 1970, Bent 1948.

Red-bellied Woodpecker *Melanerpes carolinus*

Every summer, some of this species nest near our home in southern Michigan and soon after the young are hatched, they join their parents on our suet and sunflower seed feeders. What we see happening here is also happening at many other feeders in the southern Great lakes region, and what may begin to happen in the future in more northerly areas as well. That's because the Red-bellied Woodpecker is slowly extending its range northward, to the joy of those who know this bird. It is striking, noisy, colorful, and lively—in short, a great addition to any backyard feeder system.

Redbellies are distinctively dressed, having not much red on their bellies at all, but a very obvious zebra-marked back and inner wings. Also, the males have red over the tops of their heads and down the backs of their necks, while the females have red on their necks but not on their heads. Redbellies are about Robin size, though they look longer and thinner and lower because their legs hold them closer to their perch, which is commonly the side of a tree trunk, or large tree limb. Like other woodpeckers, the Redbelly searches along tree trunks for ants, flies, caterpillars and other high-protein insects, its main dietary item.

Nests are excavated in soft or dead trees, including pines. At times, several pairs nest near one another in a loose colony. Starlings and Grackles like to take over such nests, but Redbellies are not shy and will fight for their territory, using that stout beak as a weapon. Both sexes work to dig out the nest cavity, usually a hole about 15 inches deep. The male, however, appears to do most of the work. Four or five white eggs are laid in this nest, and are incubated for about two weeks, the parents taking turns at this task. When the young hatch, they are fed partially digested seeds, insects, and fruit, the mixed diet which the parents bring to them and regurgitate into their open mouths. When the youngsters finally crawl out of the nest hole a few weeks after hatching, they already wear the distinctive black and white zebra coat given to them by their parents.

Redbellies appear to depend more heavily on a seed diet than other woodpeckers, and will commonly spend a great deal of time at our feeders munching down seeds. They also have a habit of chewing holes in fruit hanging on orchard trees, in Florida, that habit having earned them the nickname "Orange borer." Another habit of the Redbelly is to store food for future use, placing acorns, nuts, insects, and other bits of fruit in such places as crevices of fence posts and holes in trees.

In summer we hear these husky birds calling to each other in their loud *kwir, kwir, kwir* chatter. Redbellies are year-round residents of the southern Great Lakes region, and as noted above, they are slowly extending their range northward.

Key Natural History References:
Graber et al. 1977, Kilhorn 1963,
Reller 1972, Bent 1939.

Male

Female

American Robin *Turdus migratorius*

The Robin is our largest thrush, between 9 and 11 inches in body length. Most appear in the lakes states early in March. However, in winter, a few can often be found near berry trees, or beside lakes or marshy areas where temperatures are kept from the lowest extremes by the slope of a hill and the watery environment. The first Robins of spring may have been with us all winter. Those that migrate to the mid and deep south states, however, are in the majority. In March, the migrating males return about two weeks before the females. Though both sexes look much alike, males typically have darker heads than the females; both sexes sport bright breasts on their dark gray bodies.

During courtship and brood rearing the males sing their cheery song, a familiar warble that continues until July. Nests are built of grass, weeds, and string, and are carefully lined with mud and fine grass. The nest may be located as high as 70 feet above the ground, but is more often only 5 to 15 feet up. Many types of locations are used for nesting, though Robins prefer a horizontal branch or fork of a tree, a shrub, or the ledge of a building. The pale blue eggs may number from two to seven, but are usually four per nest, and these are incubated from 11 to 14 days by the female alone. After hatching, the chicks are fed in the nest for another 14 to 16 days by both parents.

As the young grow toward flight age, painted with the typical spotted breasts of the thrush family, the parents grow more and more protective. Don't be surprised if the nesting pair dive-bombs you as you approach the nest. Just back off and watch the Robin parents carry worms and insects to their young. The parents, of course, have reason to be fearful at the first-flight stage. Studies have shown that the Robin may typically be more numerous in residential areas than in the wild. Being urbanized, many robin chicks fall prey to dogs, cars, and cats at this time. The adults offset losses, however, by raising two broods each summer.

Robins are famous for their worm and insect collecting abilities, but also are notorious for the fruits they consume. Cherries and mulberries are two fruits they cherish. In winter, they devour an abundance of commercial fruits in the southern states, and are so numerous in some places they are considered pests. About 60 percent of the Robin's diet is vegetable matter, the remainder being worms, insects, and other animal protein. For a time, the chemical pesticide DDT appeared to be eliminating Robins from our midst, but since that chemical is no longer used here, Robins are back in force. It would be tragic not to have them splashing in our backyard birdbaths throughout the summer. They love to bathe, and in our yard they keep the nearby myrtle green with their splashing. They are Michigan's State Bird.

Key Natural History References:
Young 1955, Howell 1942, Graber et al. 1971, Bent 1949, Nickell 1944, Howard 1974.

Black-billed Cuckoo *Coccyzus erythropthalmus*
Yellow-billed Cuckoo *Coccyzus americanus*

These two cuckoos are much alike, but there are a few differences of plumage and habit that will help you distinguish them. First, you may expect to see either or both of these cuckoos throughout the southern portion of the Great Lakes region, but you will probably not see the Yellowbill in the Upper Peninsula or more northerly portions of our region. Second, the Yellowbill has large white spots on the underside of its brown tail, while the Blackbill has only a light colored barring on the feather ends of the tail. Third, the Yellowbill has a yellow bill—at least the lower half is yellow—while the Blackbill has a black bill. Fourth, there's a difference in the voices of the two birds. The Blackbill utters a lengthy series of soft notes, possibly up to several hundred, all of the same pitch, in groups of two or three, saying its name as it sings, *cucu, cucu, cucucu, cucucu*. The Yellowbill on the other hand clucks more than sings, and will utter a long series of notes that slow and drop in pitch at the end, as *ca, ca, ca, ca, caw, caw, cowp, cowp, cowp*.

But while either or both may nest or visit your backyard feeders, seeing cuckoos will be an event, because they are few in number and both are shy and retiring. The Blackbill prefers dense woodlands, the Yellowbill more open country. Both build their nests close to the ground in evergreens or low bushes, the Blackbill placing hers only 2 to 4 feet above ground level, the Yellowbill placing hers 6 to 8 feet up. Typically both nests are simple platforms, often flat, of sticks, twigs, and rootlets. The Blackbill female will lay 2 or 3 blue-green eggs, the Yellowbill 3 or 4 eggs, also blue-green, but a bit larger than those of the Blackbill. The females of both species also lay their eggs in the nests of other birds, and it's not uncommon to see the eggs of both cuckoos in either cuckoo nest. The little internal cuckoo thought seems to be: "Every nest needs an egg—or two, or three."

Incubation takes two weeks, and the chicks will leave their nest only a week after hatching to move about on branches near the nest. We once watched a pair of these homely youngsters, dressed in scraggly down, sit like statues in an evergreen, waiting for us to leave. After a couple weeks, the young are feathered out enough to leave the nest and search on their own for insects, berries, and other fruit which are the primary diets of both Blackbills and Yellowbills. Cuckoos will eat even the hairiest of caterpillars, types that other birds shun, research having shown that cuckoos have special digestive equipment to handle those fur coats.

Cuckoos arrive in our region in April or May and remain throughout the warm months, then head south to Central and South America when the chill winds begin to blow.

Key Natural History References: Bent 1940, Pitelka 1942, Pickens 1936.

Black-billed Cuckoo (top)   11-12 inches
Yellow-billed Cuckoo (bottom)   11-13 inches

Blue Jay *Cyanocitta cristata*

The Blue Jay, even when merely-perched on a tree limb, looks as if it were up to some mischief. It may be part of its posture that gives this impression—leaning forward, head down, looking about suspiciously. Perhaps this is because the bird itself knows that some of its habits have given it the checkered reputation it bears. This showy bird is a clown and scoffer that can move about either silently or noisily. It can be a bully at the winter feeder and is the absolute bane of any sleepy owl unlucky enough to be found lurking about in daylight. Poor Owl! Together, a gang of Blue Jays will shriek their rough, raspy *kwesh-kwesh* call, heard up to a mile and enough to keep the owl awake all day.

But the Blue Jay's behavior also leaves the impression that it is more intelligent than most. At times, it is a silent and stealthy nest robber. In winter, it dashes around with its fellow Blue Jays to any local feeder, scattering smaller birds in all directions. Then by noisy scrambling, they gorge themselves on sunflower seeds and cracked corn, looking about as if they were doing something wrong. Yet at other times, a flock of jays can move so quietly through foliage that the birdwatcher, upon discovering them, wonders how long they have been nearby.

This jay loves to hide seeds, supposedly burying them for use another time. But many solitary oaks in fields far from other oaks owe their beginnings to forgetful Blue Jays who buried acorns. These birds are larger than a Robin, ranging from 11 to 12 and one-half inches long, and are common in oak and pine woods.

The Blue Jay, despite its raw behavior, is by all counts a handsome bird. The brilliant combination of blue, black, and white plumage is the same in both sexes. The blue back and crest, whitish underparts, white spots on wings and tail, and jet black necklace distinguishes this bird from other jays. Blue Jays are most subdued in the vicinity of their nests, which the pair builds together from rough twigs and bark with a protective lining of small rootlets. The nest is built 5 to 50 feet above the ground in any handy tree—evergreen or hardwood. Both parents incubate the three to six pale olive or buff colored eggs for two weeks. Within three weeks of hatching, the young are fully fledged miniatures of their parents, but with short tails.

Originally a wild bird of the woods, Blue Jays were quick to adapt themselves to civilization, and now can be found in suburbs and cities, and also in remote oak and pine woods. They eat insects, fruit, bits of road killed carrion, seeds, and other animal and vegetable matter. Like their relative, the crow, they may be considered omnivorous.

While many Blue Jays remain in our Great Lakes region all winter, others migrate to the Gulf states for the cold season. But for most of us, enough remain behind to brighten our yards and feeders throughout the year.

Key Natural History References: Bent 1946, Goodwin 1976.

Common Grackle *Quiscalus quiscula*

Cowbirds, Starlings and Grackles are considered by many birders to be "trash birds." If they take over your feeders in spring and you'd like to discourage their presence, it's probably best to stop supplying food for a while. The Common Grackle is larger than a Robin. The males are solid black with shiny purplish heads; the females are duller colored and a little smaller than the males. Both sexes are bold, brash, and frequently a nuisance, mostly because of their great numbers. In winter they journey to gathering places in southern states, although a few will remain in Michigan's southernmost counties throughout the year. To give you an idea of the numbers of these birds, in 1978 the Christmas counters in Arkansas stated there were 10,100,000 Grackles in areas near the city of Little Rock; in 1979 the same bird watchers reported 15,100,000 grackles in the same locale during that year's Christmas count.

The males are reported to be polygamous and this may be true, because the birds nest in loose colonies of about 25 pairs in one small grove of trees or bushes. The female builds a loose structure for her nest, using grass and perhaps a lining of mud. She commonly lays five grayish eggs with dark spots and incubates them for 12 or 13 days. After the eggs hatch the male assists in transporting protein to the hungry young. We can be thankful that only one brood is hatched each summer.

A squeaky sound is the only song you hear from Grackles, yet it becomes a real din when every limb of a grove of trees supports several big birds. It is not unusual for Grackles to kill other birds; I watched a Grackle kill a sparrow with one stab of that big bill. The one I watched did not consume the sparrow, but it has been reported that some Grackles kill mice and eat them. Their diet is primarily vegetable food, but they might readily adapt to whatever food is available in a crowded environment. Unfortunately this includes the eggs and nestlings of other birds. Grackles also have the unattractive habit of following a Robin or some other bird around until it pulls up a worm, at which point the Grackle rushes in and drives the other bird away, stealing the meal.

We are happy to see the departure of the "trash" birds in the fall, but their overabundance to the south of us is causing more and more difficulty. The battle to control them will increase in intensity; watch the news for more information regarding the manner in which harassed citizens will attempt to solve the problem.

Key Natural History References:
Peterson and Young 1950, Bent 1958,
Maxwell and Putnam 1972.

Brown Thrasher *Toxostoma rufum*

Brown Thrashers will nearly always be seen near ground level. They love shrubs, hedges, and low-growing thornapple trees; in one field that we visit on our field trips, almost every isolated thornapple tree has an active thrasher nest or the remains of a nest used in previous summers. These birds use thorny twigs for the base of their bulky nest and pile grass, leaves, stems, and bark on the twig foundation. Occasionally the nest may be on the ground.

Brown Thrashers have a rich brown back and long tails and are a little longer than a Robin. Some people confuse these thrashers with any of the several brown thrushes. The brown backs and chests of both have similarities, but this Thrasher's tail is much longer, it has wing bars, and its yellow eye is easy to see. Thrashers also are larger, the largest brown thrush being about 8 inches in body length. The song of the Thrasher is not as musical as that of the thrush, but it sings loudly, and in breeding season repeats each phrase that it invents or mimics, singing each two times in rapid sequence.

Females come to us in early May about 10 days after the males have made their debut. Fussy females sometimes reject a nest site that the male has picked out. In between nest building duties and the courting process the birds might be seen scratching like chickens at any leaf-covered terrain. I've watched the leaves fly in all directions when a Thrasher is searching for a morsel of food.

Both sexes work on nest construction before the female lays four bluish-white eggs with sparse brown specks on the shell. Eggs are kept warm by both parents until the young emerge after 12 or 13 days. Both members of a pair will defend an active nest with reckless determination. The young are known to leave the nest before they are adept at flying and often encounter serious hazards in the low areas where they live. If the nest is the first brood of the summer the female may leave early to remate and start another family.

Thrashers eat oodles of beetles and grasshoppers, along with some seeds and fruit. About two thirds of their diet is insects, one third fruit and seeds. On occasion I have been able to attract them with sunflower seeds and cracked corn, but not often as they are with us at a time when plenty of rich protein food is available. However, if your backyard includes some dense bushes and is located near water or marshy areas, you may well be visited by this richly colored bird.

The Brown Thrasher is one of the group of birds that mimics the calls of other birds in a string of varied and seldom repeated notes, songs, and warbles. The group includes the Catbird and the Mockingbird.

Thrashers are common in the Lower Peninsula, less so in the Upper Peninsula. In October they leave us to reside for a time in the more "buggy" areas of our southern states, wintering from Kentucky to the Gulf.

Key Natural History References: Bent 1948, Graber et al. 1970, Erwin 1935.

11½ inches

Mourning Dove *Zenaida macroura*

Everyone is familiar with the sorrowful call of the Mourning Dove. We have been in all the states except Alaska and Hawaii and I believe we saw these doves in more places than any other species. This common bird is about the length of a Robin and has a delicate fawn color on the head and the neck; the wings are a darker color, and the pointed tail has white outer edges that are obvious when the bird flies. The sexes are alike in plumage.

In recent years more and more Mourning Doves seem to be spending their winters in the northern states. They are rarely found in the U.P. during the cold months, but they are plentiful all year round in the southern part of Michigan. In winter they are gregarious and can be seen scratching for food around many farmyards. They have also become a birdfeeder bird. The increase in number of this species has led many states to add these doves to the list of birds that can be hunted.

Mourning Dove nests are built in many kinds of trees and vines. The nest is a small platform of twigs which holds together fairly well; the twigs are so few in number that it is easily possible to see the sky through the nest. In Arizona, near Tucson, we found 20 dove nests in cholla cactus plants; the nests were only a few feet apart and the birds sat quietly as we observed them from just a few feet away. A clutch of two white eggs is normally laid, and two broods are raised each nesting season. The parents take turns warming the eggs.

After two weeks of development, the embryos emerge as helpless young; the babies are nourished with "pigeon milk" which they take as regurgitated, partially digested food by placing their bills into the beaks of the parents. In the second week the parents gradually introduce more and more whole insects into the growing youngsters' diets. At two weeks of age the young leave the nest, their new plumage being several shades of gray and brown.

In the early morning hours the doves enjoy perching on a wire, post, or tree branch and uttering their multi-syllable call: *coah, cooo, cooo, cooo*. The birds avoid the deep woods, so look for them in a stand of conifers, an old orchard, or in some suburban, open environment. Singing is most persistent in breeding season.

The Mourning Dove does not fly in flocks of thousands as the now extinct Passenger Pigeon did in the late 1800s; the extinct pigeon also had the unfortunate habit of building hundreds of nests in one tree, causing the branches to break because of the weight. Today the population of Mourning Doves remains steady, or increases from year to year depending on nesting success although hawks take their toll, and body parasites have an adverse affect on dove numbers. We hope this gentle creature stays with us for many years to come.

Key Natural History References:
Keeler 1977, Goodwin 1977, Hanson and Kossack 1962, Lehner 1965.

Mourning Dove

12 inches

Common Flicker *Colaptes auratus*

Gold shafts under the wings and tail, and the large patch of white on the rump, visible as the bird flies away, easily identify the Common Flicker, also known as the "Yellow-shafted" Flicker. Although it will stalk ground beetles, crickets, and grasshoppers, the Flicker was designed to dine on ants. It is not surprising to see it scratching about on the ground as it secures a meal of these insects, lapping them up with its "flypaper" tongue—a long, thin, sticky membrane that can sweep out a full two inches beyond the end of its bill. Avoiding the thick woods, the Flicker thrives in a habitat of partly open country where ants are easy to spot.

This bird has a large repertoire of cries and calls, but the tapping it loves to perform on trees, and its loud, repetitive *flick-a, flick-a,* will let you know it is nearby.

The brown back and the spotted gray breast of the Common Flicker contrast with the red streak on the nape of the neck and a broad, black crescent patch on the chest of both sexes. The adult male and fledglings of both sexes wear a black mustache which runs from each side of the bill. In courtship the birds sway back and forth while clinging to a tree, posing and dancing for each other. Nicknamed "high-holer," flickers prefer to nest in the upper stories of the forest. With steady, patient effort, a pair may take three weeks to chip out a chamber in a dead or dying tree, or they may find it more expedient to use an old site, or a human-placed nesting box if it suits them. This is one bird that will start a second nest to produce young in case anything happens to the first clutch of six to eight pure white eggs. One female laid an exhausting 71 eggs when a heartless experimenter, during a 73-day period, removed each one immediately after it was laid. Both parents take turns incubating the eggs for about two weeks, and the chicks remain in the chip-lined nest for three or four weeks after they hatch. The adults bring food to the young, usually ants, and thrust their long bills down the nestlings' throats to feed them the regurgitated protein.

Listed among the larger woodpeckers, Common Flickers are a rather numerous species and are easy to see and identify because of their color and size. Their flight is undulating as they first pump their powerful wings and then sail for a short distance before they pump again. These big fellows come to our birdbaths regularly, and all the other birds patiently wait for them to complete their refreshing splash in the water. To keep them nearby, provide plenty of suet attached to tree trunks. Flickers breed throughout the northern states and Canada and winter mainly in the Southwest. They can be spotted year-round in a region from the Dakotas eastward to Massachusetts and then south to the southern states. They are seen all year in the southern half of Michigan's Lower Peninsula, and throughout the rest of the state during the summer months.

Key Natural History References: Graber et al. 1977, Dennis 1969, Lawrence 1967, Bent 1939.

Mallard *Anas platyrhynchos*

The Mallard is our best known and most common duck, easily domesticated, common in parks and farmyard ponds and, in fact, the ancestor to most of our domestic ducks. The colorful male is easily recognized by his glossy green uncrested head, narrow white collar and chestnut breast. His upper parts are dark gray and under parts lighter. The center upcurled feathers in his tail are black and lent their name some years ago to a type of haircut known as the "ducktail." It was something of an insult to this bird which is handsome in its own way.

Both male and female Mallards have blue wing patches bordered on both sides by conspicuous white bars. The female at quick glance is an overall mottled brown, but she also has a dark cap and a dark streak through the eyes, plus a white tail and an orange bill. So she is almost as colorful as her mate, but in a somewhat quieter way.

Almost entirely a freshwater duck, the Mallard prefers shallow water, less than 16 inches deep, where it can feed off the bottom by tipping head down and bottom up in a method of feeding called dabbling. That makes it at home on ponds, lakes, rivers, streams and marshes throughout the the United States. It's a year-round resident of the southern Great Lakes region, and is found throughout the northern portion the entire warm season.

The staples in its diet are the seeds of sedges, grasses and smartweed, but it also eats leaves, stems, and seeds of other marsh plants, as well as snails. In addition to its pond dabbling, it will waddle over damp grassy areas and grain fields gleaning waste grain and capturing insects as it goes.

This medium to large duck, (with a body length of 20 to 28 inches and a wingspread from 30 to 40 inches) is by far the most common in the annual harvest taken by hunters in the Great Lakes region as well as by hunters nationwide. It is said to be the world's most common duck. The average annual kill in the United States alone exceeds four-and-a-half million, but even this great removal each fall tends to control rather than diminish its numbers. In fact, each spring the breeding population of Mallards is many times those which end up in the cooking pot, suggesting the great fertility of this bird.

The Mallard usually constructs a nest on the ground only a short distance from water. It is bulky, made up of grass or leaves lined with down from the female's breast. In it she lays 8 to 10 light green to white eggs at any time between March and July. There seems to be no fixed nesting period. As soon as the hatched young are dry, they are led from nest to nearby water, and they do not return to the nest thereafter.

In winter Mallards range throughout the United States south of Canada. They will remain over winter wherever there's open shallow water, and can often be seen congregating on small pools surrounded by ice.

Key Natural History References: Bellrose 1976, Palmer 1976 v. 2, Johnsgard 1975.

Female

Male

Canada Goose *Branta canadensis*

To residents of the Great Lakes states, the Canada Goose is the living symbol of wilderness in both spring and fall. The two seasons begin not by dictates of a calendar, but rather with the first long V's and deep double-syllabled calls of the "Honkers" in their classic and visible high-flying migrations. Their sounds come down from nighttime darkness, they announce their approach on clear days as well, and we earthbound humans dash outdoors to watch. Hunters await them in the fall and watchers in the spring vie to be first to announce a sighting. Almost everyone in our mid-continent region knows "the wild goose."

Its appearance, also, is familiar because many have been semi-domesticated, and because they are a favorite subject of wildlife artists and photographers. The Canada is gray-brown with a black head and neck which contrasts sharply with its light-colored breast. A white cheek patch extends under its bill to both sides of its head. The under tail feathers are white contrasting with the black tail. The sexes are alike in their coloration. Note that this bird is not called the *Canadian* Goose; a Canadian goose would be any goose found in, or migrating from, Canada, and it might be any species, wild or barnyard. This bird is always, specifically, the *Canada* Goose.

There is considerable variance in the Canada Goose's size, ranging through its numerous subspecies, but the one most common to Michigan measures about 40 inches in body length, with a wingspread of about five feet.

The Canada Goose is a vegetarian. It eats the tender shoots of grasses, sedges and other marsh plants, underwater vegetation, wild seeds and fruits and it loves to glean grain fields.

Both parents are fierce defenders of the nest, which they typically build near water in a grass-lined ground depression. Once built, they line it with body down. The pair normally mates for life and each summer raises a brood of five or six young which begin to move out of the nest with the parents the day after they are hatched. During this mid-summer period, shortly after the young hatch, the adults molt and are flightless for several weeks, and so depend on swimming for escape and mobility.

At one time, Canadas were very reduced in numbers, and continent-wide efforts were begun to help them out. As a result, in recent years, they have increased steadily throughout the continent. A surprising number of geese are captured in urban and suburban areas, to be released in rural areas, where they also thrive.

Many winter here in the Great Lakes region wherever there's open water and sufficient feeding sites and agricultural lands to provide grazing. But whether they migrate or winter-over, this large, strong bird is a favorite with all birders.

Key Natural History References: Palmer 1976 v. 2, Johnsgard 1975, Bellrose 1976.

Ring-necked Pheasant *Phasianus colchicus*

This imported pheasant is over two feet long, but much of that measurement is the long tail. Many areas of the United States have tried to raise a population of this game bird but they thrive only in the northern states. The density of the pheasant population varies greatly from region to region in states where they are found, perhaps because usable pheasant cover along roads and edges of fields is diminishing in some areas but holding its own in others. Michigan was once a national leader in pheasant production, but in recent years numbers have dwindled here.

Male pheasants are colorful, almost gawdy birds. They have a red-brown back and chest and an iridescent green head. Around their eyes are red patches that are not feathered, and a white collar circles their necks. Gray and tan on the wings and tail of the male add to his colorful coat. The female has a gray-brown body with a light colored eye-ring; she has a shorter tail than the male and her earthy colors enable her to conceal herself readily during nesting season.

During mating season the male struts about in front of the females and raises his feathery ear tufts. After mating, the female will typically build her nest in a field or in heavy growth under a fence. She lays about a dozen eggs in the well hidden, grassy nest. For three and a half weeks she sits so tightly on the nest that she will not move until she is under the foot of an intruder. The olive-brown eggs hatch after 24 days and the young have a mixture of rust and brown down that helps them hide when necessary. The young are able to run rapidly almost as soon as they are out of the egg. They learn to fly at a very early age, though not well at first.

Adult pheasants often frequent grain fields where they can glean corn and wheat of the harvest. Babies eat insects in great numbers when they first start following the mother across the fields. Most of us have seen the parade of a pheasant family; use caution as you drive if you see the mother enter the roadway in breeding season. It's fun to park and watch one baby after another emerge from the tall weeds to dash across the road and join the adult family.

Pheasants are superb runners and spend many hours roaming the countryside; their flight is often for short distances in a straight line. Hunters love to bag their limit of these birds because they provide such good fare. For several years Michigan's Ottawa County along the shore of Lake Michigan was prime pheasant territory. This has not been the case in the past few years. In fact, a few years ago, the crowing of pheasants nearly disappeared from many areas, so if you do see a few of these colorful game birds near your home try to make them happy in winter with an abundant supply of corn.

Key Natural History References: Allen 1956, Bent 1932, Gould 1940.

Male

Female

About Feeders And Feeding

When selecting a birdfeeder, it is important that you determine what you expect out of your feeding station. For instance, many bird specialists recommend that if a person is going to have only one feeder, it might best be a *feeding platform.* This type is open on at least two sides but with a roof forming a protective overhang. A feeding platform can be mounted on a pipe or suspended by a wire on a tree branch. When suspended, its only disadvantage is that it does not perform well in high winds.

Two of the most common specialty feeders are the clear plastic tube feeder, and the bubble feeder. Bubble feeders are small and do not have any perches while tube feeders have perches. Tube feeders are designed for small birds; however, with the addition of a seed-catching tray larger birds also can be accommodated. With the tube feeder, seed is dispensed through feeding ports or small holes in the plastic. They may have either large openings for sunflower seeds or small openings containing niger (thistle) seeds. A tube design insures bird safety because the bird can stay outside the feeder while eating. The food, in turn, is on the inside protected from weather and bird droppings.

The dome feeder, another type of specialty feeder, hopes to conquer the battle between squirrels and bird lovers. A dome feeder is a large inverted rounded bowl suspended over a smaller bowl or tray. The idea is that the dome will tilt when squirrels hop on to reach the seed in the tray beneath and that causes them to slide off unharmed. But some birdwatchers report that inventive squirrels even find ways to get seeds out of dome feeders, so you might have to revert to a feeder known as the Hylarious, which has a trapdoor that drops down to cover the seeds whenever the weight of a squirrel lands on the feeder. The door lifts out of the way exposing the seed to the smaller, lightweight birds as soon as the squirrel leaves. Hylarious Feeders are advertised in various publications including, usually, *Audubon Magazine,* normally available at major newsstands and in most public libraries. There may be other commercial types of trapdoor feeders available as well in the near future. Window feeders, a type that can be filled from indoors, are popular with shut-ins, apartment dwellers, the elderly, and anyone who is unable to get outside on a regular basis.

You can also construct your own feeder, using wood, lucite, metal, thick glass, or other common household materials. A free hopper feeder can be made from an old milk carton. On each of the four corners, an inch or two above the bottom, make a single horizontal cut into a clean milk carton as shown in the

sketch. Push in the cardboard corners as shown to expose a little tray-like area inside the carton. Then punch holes in the four bottom corners and run sticks or dowels through the holes to serve as perches. Fill the carton with sunflower seeds, white millet, cracked corn, or thistle (niger) seeds, or any mixture of these, and hang the carton from a porch eave, tree branch, or other location where it can be seen from a window.

Suet is another easy way to attract birds. You can hang large lumps of plain suet in onion sacks against the trunk of a tree, or suspended from a tree limb, or you can melt the suet, mix in a lot of seeds, then as it cools form the hardening suet into a softball-sized ball and hang it outside in an onion sack.

The ground itself should not be ignored as a feeding station. Sparrows, juncos, and towhees actually prefer food right on the ground. Split logs can be used to form a trough which prevents food from blowing away. Dried corn on the cob, set upright on nails driven into a board, is another popular ground feeder. It is easy to make by simply driving spikes into a slightly elevated board. You can press the corn cobs upright onto the spikes by hand. However, be sure to place all ground feeders in the open where birds can see approaching cats or dogs.

Recently, a great deal of study has been made on the kinds of food preferred by various species of birds. This data indicates that oil (black) sunflower seeds are the most popular seed with most seed-eating birds and particularly with birds attracted to elevated feeders. White millet appears to be the most popular seed among several sparrows and other ground feeding birds. Niger, or thistle seed, is popular with many small birds, especially goldfinches. Although expensive, the seeds are small, so a 10 pound bag provides thousands of seeds that last a relatively long time in feeders.

Unfortunately, if bird lovers do not handle seed properly many avian diseases can be spread. Feeders should be cleaned regularly, seed should be kept fresh and dry and stored in garbage cans or other watertight containers, and moldy feed should be buried or burned. The ground feeding area also should be cleaned periodically to remove rotten seed, an act which will help guard against disease.

Feeder location is another important consideration. A feeder should be near a small bush or tree so the birds can fly to safe locations and survey the area before flying to the feeder perch. If you have a feeder placed near a glass window remember that large picture windows frequently reflect the landscape and bewilder a bird, causing it to fly against the glass. Many people prevent this by placing decals on their windows, by closing curtains during glare-prone periods of the day, or by hanging streamers.

In addition to feeding birds, it is important to provide a water source. Birds are especially appreciative of water during the winter and will sometimes pass up feed for a bird bath. It is important never to use chemicals, such as anti-freeze, in your bird bath. Instead, to prevent freezing, small heaters can be purchased or a shallow pan of water can be placed out in the yard with a light bulb lit under the pan and surrounded by insulation.

As your interest in bird watching continues to grow, you'll find new ways to attract birds to your window. We all still have a lot to learn, but fortunately the enjoyment continues to increase with the effort and knowledge produced.

151

Checklist Of Birds In This Book

☐ BLACKBIRD, RED-WINGED
Agelaius phoeniceus
When _____
Where _____

☐ BLUEBIRD, EASTERN
Sialia sialis
When _____
Where _____

☐ BOBOLINK
Dolichonyx oryzivorus
When _____
Where _____

☐ BUNTING, INDIGO
Passerina cyanea
When _____
Where _____

☐ CARDINAL, NORTHERN
Cardinalis cardinalis
When _____
Where _____

☐ CATBIRD, GRAY
Dumetella carolinensis
When _____
Where _____

☐ CHICKADEE, BLACK-CAPPED
Parus atricapillus
When _____
Where _____

☐ COWBIRD, BROWN-HEADED
Molothrus ater
When _____
Where _____

☐ CREEPER, BROWN
Certhia familiaris
When _____
Where _____

☐ CUCKOO, BLACK-BILLED
Coccyzus erythropthalmus
When _____
Where _____

☐ CUCKOO, YELLOW-BILLED
Coccyzus americanus
When _____
Where _____

☐ DOVE, MOURNING
Zenaida macroura
When _____
Where _____

☐ DUCK, MALLARD
Anas platyrhynchos
When _____
Where _____

☐ FINCH, PURPLE
Carpodacus purpureus
When _____
Where _____

☐ FLICKER, COMMON
Colaptes auratus
When _____
Where _____

☐ FLYCATCHER, ALDER
Empidonax alnorum
When _____
Where _____

☐ FLYCATCHER, GREAT CRESTED
Myiarchus crinitus
When _____
Where _____

☐ FLYCATCHER, LEAST
Empidonax minimus
When _____
Where _____

☐ FLYCATCHER, WILLOW
Empidonax traillii
When _____
Where _____

☐ GNATCATCHER, BLUE-GRAY
Polioptila caerulea
When _____
Where _____

☐ GOLDFINCH, AMERICAN
Carduelis tristis
When _____
Where _____

☐ GOOSE, CANADA
Branta canadensis
When _____
Where _____

☐ GRACKLE, COMMON
Quiscalus quiscula
When _____
Where _____

☐ GROSBEAK, EVENING
Hesperiphona vespertina
When _____
Where _____

□ GROSBEAK, PINE
Pinicola enucleator
When _____
Where _____

□ GROSBEAK ROSE-BREASTED
Pheucticus ludovicianus
When _____
Where _____

□ HUMMINGBIRD, RUBY-THROATED
Archilochus colubris
When _____
Where _____

□ JAY, BLUE
Cyanocitta cristata
When _____
Where _____

□ JUNCO, NORTHERN
Junco hyemalis
When _____
Where _____

□ KINGBIRD, EASTERN
Tyrannus tyrannus
When _____
Where _____

□ KINGLET, GOLDEN-CROWNED
Regulus satrapa
When _____
Where _____

□ KINGLET, RUBY-CROWNED
Regulus calendula
When _____
Where _____

□ LARK, HORNED
Eremophila alpestris
When _____
Where _____

□ MARTIN, PURPLE
Progne subis
When _____
Where _____

□ NUTHATCH, RED-BREASTED
Sitta canadensis
When _____
Where _____

□ NUTHATCH, WHITE-BREASTED
Sitta carolinensis
When _____
Where _____

□ ORIOLE, NORTHERN "BALTIMORE"
Icterus galbula
When _____
Where _____

□ OVENBIRD
Seiurus aurocapillus
When _____
Where _____

□ PEEWEE, EASTERN WOOD
Contopus virens
When _____
Where _____

□ PHEASANT, RING-NECKED
Phasianus colchicus
When _____
Where _____

□ PHOEBE, EASTERN
Sayornis phoebe
When _____
Where _____

□ REDPOLL, COMMON
Carduelis flammea
When _____
Where _____

□ REDSTART, AMERICAN
Setophaga ruticilla
When _____
Where _____

□ ROBIN, AMERICAN
Turdus migratorius
When _____
Where _____

□ SAPSUCKER, YELLOW-BELLIED
Sphyrapicus varius
When _____
Where _____

□ SISKIN, PINE
Carduelis pinus
When _____
Where _____

□ SPARROW, AMERICAN TREE
Spizella arborea
When _____
Where _____

□ SPARROW, CHIPPING
Spizella passerina
When _____
Where _____

□ SPARROW, FIELD
Spizella pusilla
When _____
Where _____

□ SPARROW, HOUSE
Passer domesticus
When _____
Where _____

□ SPARROW, SONG
Melospiza melodia
When _____
Where _____

□ SPARROW, SWAMP
Melospiza georgiana
When _____
Where _____

☐ SPARROW, WHITE-THROATED
Zonotrichia albicollis
When _____
Where _____

☐ STARLING, EUROPEAN
Sturnis vulgaris
When _____
Where _____

☐ SWALLOW, BARN
Hirundo rustica
When _____
Where _____

☐ SWALLOW, TREE
Iridoprocne bicolor
When _____
Where _____

☐ SWIFT, CHIMNEY
Chaetura pelagica
When _____
Where _____

☐ TANAGER, SCARLET
Piranga olivacea
When _____
Where _____

☐ THRASHER, BROWN
Toxostoma rufum
When _____
Where _____

☐ THRUSH, HERMIT
Catharus guttatus
When _____
Where _____

☐ THRUSH, WOOD
Hylocichla mustelina
When _____
Where _____

☐ TITMOUSE, TUFTED
Parus bicolor
When _____
Where _____

☐ TOWHEE, RUFOUS-SIDED
Pipilo erythrophthalmus
When _____
Where _____

☐ VIREO, RED-EYED
Vireo olivaceus
When _____
Where _____

☐ WARBLER, BLACK & WHITE
Mniotilta varia
When _____
Where _____

☐ WARBLER, NASHVILLE
Vermivora ruficapilla
When _____
Where _____

☐ WARBLER, TENNESSEE
Vermivora peregrina
When _____
Where _____

☐ WARBLER, YELLOW
Dendroica petechia
When _____
Where _____

☐ WARBLER, YELLOW-RUMPED
Dendroica coronata
When _____
Where _____

☐ WAXWING, CEDAR
Bombycilla cedrorum
When _____
Where _____

☐ WOODPECKER, DOWNY
Picoides pubescens
When _____
Where _____

☐ WOODPECKER, HAIRY
Picoides villosus
When _____
Where _____

☐ WOODPECKER RED-BELLIED
Melanerpes carolinus
When _____
Where _____

☐ WOODPECKER, RED-HEADED
Melanerpes erythrocephalus
When _____
Where _____

☐ WREN, HOUSE
Troglodytes aedon
When _____
Where _____

☐ WREN, MARSH
Cistothorus palustris
When _____
Where _____

☐ YELLOWTHROAT, COMMON
Geothlypis trichas
When _____
Where _____

Checklist Of All Michigan Birds

The following list of 405 birds known to nest or migrate through or visit Michigan was compiled by Robert B. Payne of the University of Michigan's Museum of Zoology. It represents records of museum specimens, field observations, photos, and tape recordings through early 1982, and extending back to earliest reports. You'll note in a handful of cases differences of common names for some species; the book itself listing one name, the checklist another. Species in the book follow the earlier, more commonly known, species names established by the American Ornithologists' Union (AOU) prior to about 1975; checklist includes changes made in the last 8 to 10 years, and in use primarily by specialists.

____Anhinga
____Ani, Groove-billed
____Ani, Smooth-billed
____Avocet, American
____Bittern, American
____Bittern, Least
____Blackbird, Brewer's
____Blackbird, Red-winged
____Blackbird, Rusty
____Blackbird, Yellow-headed
____Bluebird, Eastern
____Bluebird, Mountain
____Bobolink
____Bobwhite, Northern
____Brant
____Bufflehead
____Bunting, Indigo
____Bunting, Lark
____Bunting, Painted
____Bunting, Snow
____Canvasback
____Caracara, Crested
____Cardinal, Northern
____Catbird, Gray
____Chat, Yellow-breasted
____Chickadee, Black-capped
____Chickadee, Boreal
____Chickadee, Carolina
____Chuck-will's-widow
____Coot, American
____Cormorant, Double-crested
____Cowbird, Brown-headed
____Crane, Sandhill
____Creeper, Brown
____Crow, American
____Crossbill, Red

____Crossbill, White-winged
____Cuckoo, Black-billed
____Cuckoo, Yellow-billed
____Curlew, Eskimo
____Curlew, Long-billed
____Dickcissel
____Dove, Common Ground
____Dove, Mourning
____Dove, Rock
____Dovekie
____Dowitcher, Long-billed
____Dowitcher, Short-billed
____Duck, American Black
____Duck, Black-bellied Whistling
____Duck, Fulvous Whistling
____Duck, Harlequin
____Duck, Ring-necked
____Duck, Ruddy
____Duck, Tufted
____Duck, Wood
____Dunlin
____Eagle, Bald
____Eagle, Golden
____Egret, Cattle
____Egret, Great
____Egret, Snowy
____Eider, Common
____Eider, King
____Falcon, Peregrine
____Falcon, Prairie
____Finch, House
____Finch, Purple
____Finch, Rosy
____Flamingo, Greater

____Flicker, Northern
____Flycatcher, Acadian
____Flycatcher, Alder
____Flycatcher, Great Crested
____Flycatcher, Least
____Flycatcher, Olive-sided
____Flycatcher, Scissor-tailed
____Flycatcher, Vermillion
____Flycatcher, Willow
____Flycatcher, Yellow-bellied
____Gadwall
____Gallinule, Purple
____Gannet, Northern
____Gannet, Blue-gray
____Godwit, Hudsonian
____Godwit, Marbled
____Goldeneye, Barrow's
____Goldeneye, Common
____Goldfinch, American
____Goldfinch, European
____Goose, Bar-headed
____Goose, Barnacle
____Goose, Canada
____Goose, Greater White-fronted
____Goose, Ross'
____Goose, Snow
____Goshawk, Northern
____Grackle, Common
____Grebe, Eared
____Grebe, Horned
____Grebe, Pied-billed
____Grebe, Red-necked
____Grebe, Western
____Grosbeak, Black-headed
____Grosbeak, Blue

_____Grosbeak, Evening
_____Grosbeak, Pine
_____Grosbeak,
    Rose-breasted
_____Grouse, Ruffed
_____Grouse, Sharp-tailed
_____Grouse, Spruce
_____Gull, Bonaparte's
_____Gull, California
_____Gull, Common
    Black-headed
_____Gull, Franklin's
_____Gull, Glaucous
_____Gull, Glaucous-winged
_____Gull, Great
    Black-backed
_____Gull, Heermann's
_____Gull, Herring
_____Gull, Iceland
_____Gull, Ivory
_____Gull, Laughing
_____Gull, Lesser
    Black-backed
_____Gull, Little
_____Gull, Mew
_____Gull, Ring-billed
_____Gull, Sabine's
_____Gull, Thayer's
_____Gyrfalcon
_____Harrier, Northern
_____Hawk, Broad-winged
_____Hawk, Cooper's
_____Hawk, Ferruginous
_____Hawk,
    Red-shouldered
_____Hawk, Red-tailed
_____Hawk, Rough-legged
_____Hawk, Sharp-shinned
_____Hawk, Swainson's
_____Heron, Black-crowned
_____Heron, Great Blue
_____Heron, Green
_____Heron, Little Blue
_____Heron, Louisiana
_____Heron, Yellow-
    crowned Night
_____Hummingbird,
    Ruby-throated
_____Hummingbird, Rufous
_____Ibis, Glossy
_____Ibis, White
_____Ibis, White-faced
_____Jaeger, Long-tailed
_____Jaeger, Parasitic
_____Jaeger, Pomarine
_____Jay, Blue
_____Jay, Gray
_____Junco, Dark-eyed

_____Kestrel, American
_____Killdeer
_____Kingbird, Eastern
_____Kingbird, Western
_____Kingfisher, Belted
_____Kinglet,
    Golden-crowned
_____Kinglet,
    Ruby-crowned
_____Kite, American
    Swallow-tailed
_____Kite, Black-shouldered
_____Kite, Mississippi
_____Kittiwake,
    Black-legged
_____Knot, Red
_____Lark, Horned
_____Longspur,
    Chestnut-collared
_____Longspur, Lapland
_____Longspur, McCown's
_____Longspur, Smith's
_____Loon, Common
_____Loon, Red-throated
_____Magpie, Black-billed
_____Mallard
_____Martin, Purple
_____Meadowlark, Eastern
_____Meadowlark, Western
_____Merganser, Common
_____Merganser, Hooded
_____Merganser,
    Red-breasted
_____Merlin
_____Mockingbird,
    Northern
_____Moorhen, Common
_____Murre, Thick-billed
_____Murrelet, Ancient
_____Nighthawk, Common
_____Nutcracker, Clarke's
_____Nuthatch,
    Red-breasted
_____Nuthatch,
    White-breasted
_____Oldsquaw
_____Oriole, Audubon's
_____Oriole, Hooded
_____Oriole, Northern
_____Oriole, Orchard
_____Osprey
_____Ovenbird
_____Owl, Barred
_____Owl, Boreal
_____Owl, Burrowing
_____Owl, Common Barn
_____Owl, Eastern Screech
_____Owl, Great Gray

_____Owl, Great Horned
_____Owl, Long-eared
_____Owl, Northern Hawk
_____Owl, Northern
    Saw-whet
_____Owl, Short-eared
_____Owl, Snowy
_____Parakeet, Carolina
_____Parakeet, Monk
_____Partridge, Gray
_____Parula, Northern
_____Pelican, American
    White
_____Pelican, Brown
_____Phalarope, Red
_____Phalarope, Red-
    necked
_____Phalarope, Wilson's
_____Pheasant, Ring-necked
_____Phoebe, Eastern
_____Phoebe, Say's
_____Pigeon, Band-tailed
_____Pigeon, Passenger
_____Pintail, Northern
_____Pipit, Sprague's
_____Pipit, Water
_____Plover, Black-bellied
_____Plover, Lesser Golden
_____Plover, Piping
_____Plover, Semipalmated
_____Plover, Snowy
_____Prairie-Chicken,
    Greater
_____Ptarmigan, Willow
_____Rail, Black
_____Rail, King
_____Rail, Virginia
_____Rail, Yellow
_____Raven, Common
_____Redhead
_____Redpoll, Common
_____Redpoll, Hoary
_____Redstart, American
_____Robin, American
_____Ruff
_____Sanderling
_____Sandpiper, Baird's
_____Sandpiper,
    Buff-breasted
_____Sandpiper, Curlew
_____Sandpiper, Least
_____Sandpiper, Pectoral
_____Sandpiper, Purple
_____Sandpiper,
    Semipalmated
_____Sandpiper, Solitary
_____Sandpiper, Spotted
_____Sandpiper, Stilt

____Sandpiper, Upland
____Sandpiper, Western
____Sandpiper,
     White-rumped
____Sapsucker,
     Yellow-bellied
____Scaup, Greater
____Scaup, Lesser
____Scoter, Black
____Scoter, Surf
____Scoter, White-winged
____Shoveler, Northern
____Shrike, Loggerhead
____Shrike, Northern
____Siskin, Pine
____Skimmer, Black
____Snipe, Common
____Solitaire, Townsend's
____Sora
____Sparrow, American
     Tree
____Sparrow, Bachman's
____Sparrow, Chipping
____Sparrow, Clay-colored
____Sparrow, Field
____Sparrow, Fox
____Sparrow,
     Golden-crowned
____Sparrow, Grasshopper
____Sparrow, Harris'
____Sparrow, Henslow's
____Sparrow, House
____Sparrow, Lark
____Sparrow, Le Conte's
____Sparrow, Lincoln's
____Sparrow, Savannah
____Sparrow, Sharp-tailed
____Sparrow, Song
____Sparrow, Swamp
____Sparrow, Vesper
____Sparrow,
     White-crowned
____Sparrow,
     White-throated
____Starling, European
____Stilt, Black-necked
____Stork, Wood
____Swallow, Bank
____Swallow, Barn
____Swallow, Cliff
____Swallow, Northern
     Rough-winged
____Swallow, Tree
____Swan, Mute
____Swan, Trumpeter
____Swan, Tundra
____Swift, Chimney
____Swift, White-throated

____Tanager, Scarlet
____Tanager, Summer
____Tanager, Western
____Teal, Blue-winged
____Teal, Cinnamon
____Teal, Green-winged
____Tern, Arctic
____Tern, Black
____Tern, Caspian
____Tern, Common
____Tern, Forster's
____Tern, Least
____Thrasher, Brown
____Thrasher, Curve-billed
____Thrush, Gray-cheeked
____Thrush, Hermit
____Thrush, Swainson's
____Thrush, Varied
____Thrush, Wood
____Titmouse, Tufted
____Towhee, Green-tailed
____Towhee, Rufous-sided
____Turkey, Wild
____Turnstone, Ruddy
____Veery
____Vireo, Bell's
____Vireo, Philadelphia
____Vireo, Red-eyed
____Vireo, Solitary
____Vireo, Warbling
____Vireo, White-eyed
____Vireo, Yellow-throated
____Vulture, Black
____Vulture, Turkey
____Warbler, Bay-breasted
____Warbler,
     Black-and-white
____Warbler, Black-
     throated Blue
____Warbler, Black-
     throated Gray
____Warbler, Black-
     throated Green
____Warbler, Blackburnian
____Warbler, Blackpoll
____Warbler, Blue-winged
____Warbler, Canada
____Warbler, Cape May
____Warbler, Cerulean
____Warbler,
     Chestnut-sided
____Warbler, Connecticut
____Warbler,
     Golden-winged
____Warbler, Hooded
____Warbler, Kentucky
____Warbler, Kirtland's
____Warbler, Magnolia

____Warbler, Mourning
____Warbler, Nashville
____Warbler,
     Orange-crowned
____Warbler, Palm
____Warbler, Pine
____Warbler, Prairie
____Warbler,
     Prothonotary
____Warbler, Tennessee
____Warbler, Wilson's
____Warbler, Worm-eating
____Warbler, Yellow
____Warbler,
     Yellow-rumped
____Warbler,
     Yellow-throated
____Waterthrush,
     Louisiana
____Waterthrush,
     Northern
____Waxwing, Bohemian
____Waxwing, Cedar
____Wheatear, Northern
____Whimbrel,
____Whip-poor-will
____Wigeon, American
____Wigeon, Eurasian
____Willet
____Wood-pewee, Eastern
____Woodcock, American
____Woodpecker,
     Black-backed
____Woodpecker, Downy
____Woodpecker,
     Golden-fronted
____Woodpecker, Hairy
____Woodpecker, Lewis
____Woodpecker, Pileated
____Woodpecker,
     Red-bellied
____Woodpecker,
     Red-cockaded
____Woodpecker, Red-
     headed
____Woodpecker,
     Three-toed
____Wren, Bewick's
____Wren, Carolina
____Wren, House
____Wren, Marsh
____Wren, Rock
____Wren, Sedge
____Wren, Winter
____Yellowlegs, Greater
____Yellowlegs, Lesser
____Yellowthroat,
     Common

Bibliography

Allen, A.A., 1933a. The Crested Flycatcher's story. Bird-Lore 35(4):285-293. 1933b.The Indigo Bunting. Bird-Lore 35:227-235.

Allen, D. (ed.), 1956. Pheasants in N.A. The Stackpole Co., Harrisburg, PA & the Wildl. Mgmt. Inst., Wash., D.C. 490p.

Allen, R.W., and Nice, M.M., 1952. Breeding biology of Purple Martin. Am. Midl. Nat. 47(3):606-665.

Andrle, R.F., 1971. Range extension of Golden-crowned Kinglet in N.Y. Wilson Bull. 83:313-316.

Belknap, J.B., 1973. The Evening Grosbeak in N.Y. State. Kingbird 23:122-124

Bellrose, F.C., 1976. Ducks, geese, & swans of N.A. Stackpole Books, Harrisburg, Penn. 540p.

Bent, A.C., 1932-1968. Life Histories of N.A. Birds, in 26 volumes. First published as bulletins of Natl. Mus. through 1968, subsequently published by Dover Press, N.Y. as a series of paperbacks, some are still available from the publisher.

Bertin, R.I., 1977. Breeding habitats of Wood Thrush & Veery. Condor 79(3):303-311.

Best, L.B., 1977. Territory quality & mating in the Field Sparrow. Condor 79(2):192-203. 1978. Field Sparrow reproduction & nesting ecology. Auk 95(1):9-22.

Bowdish, B.S., and Phillipp, P.B., 1916. The Tennessee Warbler in New Brunswick. Auk 33:1-8.

Boyd, E.M., 1962. A half-century's changes in birdlife near Springfield, Mass. Bird-Banding 33:137-148.

Bradley, H.L., 1948. A life history of the Indigo Bunting. Jack-Pine Warbler 26:103-113.

Breckenridge, W.J., 1956. Measurements of the habitat of Least Flycatcher. Wilson Bull. 68:47-51.

Brewer, R., 1961. Notes on the life history of the Carolina Chickadee. Wilson Bull. 73:348-373.

Butts, W.K., 1931. Study of Chickadee & White-breasted Nuthatch. Bird-Banding 2:1-26.

Case, N.A., and Hewitt, O.H., 1963. Nesting of the Red-winged Blackbird. Living Bird 2:7-20.

Conner, R.N., 1976. Nesting of Red-headed Woodpeckers in southwestern VA. Bird-Banding 47:40-43.

Crooks, M.P., 1948. Life history of Field Sparrow, M.S. Thesis, Iowa State College, Ames.

Davis, E.M., 1937. Observations on nesting Barn Swallows. Bird-Banding 8:66-73.

Davis, J., 1960. Nesting of the Rufous-sided Towhee in coastal Calif. Condor 62:434-456.

Dennis, J.V., 1969. Yellow-shafted Flicker on Nantucket Island, Mass. Bird-Banding 40(4):290-308.

Dexter, R.W., 1977. Synopsis of 1976 season for Chimney Swifts at Kent State University. Bird-Banding 48(1):73-74

Dilger, W.C., 1956. The Hermit & Wood Thrushes.Wilson Bull. 68(3):171-199.

Dow, D.D., 1969. Range & habitat of Cardinal. Can. J. of Zool. 47:103-115.

Dunnett, G.M., 1955. Breeding of European Starling in relation to food supply. Ibis 97:619-662

Erwin, W.G., 1935. Nesting habits of the Brown Thrasher. Jour. Tenn. Acad. Sci. 10:179-204

Findlay, J.C., 1971. Breeding of Purple Martins at northern range. Wilson Bull. 83(3):255-269.

Fischer, R.B., 1958. Breeding of Chimney Swift. N.Y. State Mus. & Sci. Serv. Bull. 368. 141p.

Fischer, R.B., and Gills, G., 1946. Study of White-throated Sparrow. Auk 63:402-418.

Forbush, E.H., 1929. Birds of Mass. & other New England States, 3 vol. Mass. Dept. of Ag.

Fretwell, S., 1969. Behavior & winter habitat of Juncos. Bird-Banding 40(1):1-25.

Friedmann, H., 1929. the Cowbirds. C.C. Thomas, Springfield, Ill. 421p.

Gabrielson, I.N., 1915. Field observations of Rose-breasted Grosbeak. Wilson Bull. 27:357-368.

Gillespie, M., 1930. Behavior & distribution of Tufted Titmouse in winter & spring. Bird-Banding 1:113-126.

Goodwin, D., 1976. Crows of the World. Cornell Univ. Press, Ithaca, N.Y. 359p. 1977. Pigeons & Doves of the World. 2nd ed. Cornell Univ. Press, Ithaca, N.Y. 446p.

Gould, E.W., 1940. Study of Pheasant in N.H. during spring & early summer. N.H. Fish & Game Dept., Concord. 10p, mimeo.

Graber, et al. 1970-1977. Ill. Nat. Hist. Surv. Biol. Notes.

Griscom, L., and Sprunt A., Jr., 1957. Warblers of America. Devin-Adair Co., N.Y. 356p.

Hann, H.W., 1937. Life history of Ovenbird in southern Mich. Wilson Bull. 49(3)145-237.

Hanson, H.C., and Kossack, C.W., 1962. Mourning Dove in Ill. Southern Ill. Univ. Press, Carbondale. 133p.

Harrison, H., 1975. Field guide to bird's nests east of Miss. River, Houghton Mifflin, Boston. 350p.

Hartshorne, J.M., 1962. Behavior of Eastern Bluebird at nest. The Living Bird 1:131-149.

Hespenheide, H.A., 1971. Flycatcher habitat in eastern deciduous forest. Auk 88(1):61-74.

Howard, D.V., 1977. Urban Robins population study. pp. 67-75. Plan. & Res. Div. Ser. 28, Holdsworth Nat. Res. Center, Univ. Of Mass., Amherst.

Howell, J.C., 1942. Nesting habits of American Robin. Am. Midl. Nat. 28:529-603.

Howell, T.R., 1952. Natl. history & differences in Yellow-bellied Sapsucker. Condor 54:237-282.

James, R.D., 1976. Foraging & habitat of three vireo species in southern Ontario. Wilson Bull. 88:62-75.

Johnsgard, P.A., 1975. Waterfowl of N.A., Indiana Univ. Press. Bloomington. 575p.

Johnston, D.W., 1971. Niche relationships among flycatchers. Auk 88:796-804.

Kale, H.W.II., 1965. Ecology & bioenergetics of long-billed Marsh Wren in Georgia salt marshes. Nuttall Ornith. Club Publ. No. 5, Cambridge, Mass. 142p.

Keeler, J.E., 1977. Mourning Dove. 275-298pp. Mgmt of Migratory Shore & Upland Game Birds in N.A. Internatl. Assoc. of Fish & Wildl. Agencies. Wash. DC. 358p.

Kendeigh, S.C., 1941b. Territorial & mating behavior of House Wren. Univ. of Ill. Biol. Mongr. 18(3):1-120.

Kessel, B., 1957. Breeding of European Starling in N.A. Am. Midl. Nat. 58(2):257-331.

Kilham, L., 1962. Breeding of Yellow-bellied Sapsuckers. Auk 79:31-43. 1963. Food storing of Red-bellied Woodpeckers. Wilson Bull. 75(3):227-234 1968b. Reproductive behavior of White-breasted Nuthatch. Auk 85(3):477-492.

King, J.R., 1955. Life history of Traill's (Willow) Flycatcher. Auk 72:148-173.

Kluyver, H.M., 1961. Food consumption & habitat in breeding Chickadees. Auk 78:532-550.

Kuerzi, R.G., 1941. Life history of Tree Swallow. Proc. Linn. Soc. No. 52-3. 1-52pp.

Laskey, A.R., 1940. Nesting season of Bluebirds at Nashville, Tenn. Wilson Bull. 52:183-190. 1944. Study of Cardinal in Tenn. Wilson Bull. 56:27-44 1957. Life history of Tufted Titmouse. Bird-Banding 28:135-144.

Lawrence, L. de K., 1948. Comparative study of nesting behavior of Chestnut-sided & Nashville Warblers, Auk 65:204-219. 1952. Redbreast makes a home. Audubon Mag. 54:16-21. 1953. Nesting & behavior of Red-eyed Vireo. The Can. Field Nat. 67(2):47-77. 1967. Life history of four woodpecker species. Ornith. Mono. No. 5. Am. Ornith. Union, Lawrence, KA. 156p.

Lea, R.B., 1942. Study of nesting habits of Cedar Waxwing. Wilson Bull. 54:225-237.

Lehner, P.N., 1965. Observations in N.Y. on ecology of Mourning Dove. N.Y. Fish & Game J. 12:147-169.

Lepthien, L.W., and Bock, C.E., 1976. Winter patterns of N.A. Kinglets. Wilson Bull. 88(3):483-485.

Longcore, J.R., and Jones, R.E., 1969. Reproduction of Wood Thrush in Delaware wood lot. Wilson Bull. 81:396-406.

MacArthur, R.H., 1958. Population of warblers of northeastern coniferous forest. Ecology 39(4):599-619.

MacQueen, P.M., 1950. Territory & song in Least Flycatcher. Wilson Bull. 62:194-205.

Martin, N.D., 1960. Bird population in relation to forest succession Algonquin Prov. Park, Ont. Ecology 41:126-140.

Maxwell, G.R. II, and Putnam L.S., 1972. Incubation of young & nests of Common Grackle in northern Ohio. Auk 89(2):349-359.

Morse, D.H., 1972. Habitat diff. of Swainson's and Hermit Thrush. Wilson Bull. 84(2):206-208. 1976. Variables in density & territory of breeding spruce-wood warblers. Ecology 57(2):290-301.

Mousley, H., 1934. Study of Northern Crested Flycatcher. Auk 51:207-216.

Nice, M.M., 1932. Nesting of Blue-gray Gnatcatcher. Condor 34:18-22.

1937. Life history of Song Sparrow I. Trans. of Linn. Soc. Of N.Y. 4:1-247.

1943. Life history of Song Sparrow II. Trans. of Linn. Soc. of N.Y. 6:1-328.

Nickell, W.P., 1944. Habitat studies of Robin nests. Jack-Pine Warbler 22(2):48-64.

1951. Habitat studies of Eastern Goldfinch. Auk 68:447-470.

1965. Habitat studies of Catbird. Am. Midl. Nat. 73:433-478.

North, C.A., 1972. Population dynamics of House Sparrow in Wisc. 195-210pp.

Odum, E.P., 1941. Annual cycle of Black-capped Chickadees. Auk 58:314-333, 518-535.

1942. Annual cycle of Black-capped Chickadees. Auk 59(4):499-531.

Odum, E.P., & Johnston, D.W., 1951. House Wren breeding in Georgia. Auk 68:357-366.

Orians, G.H., 1961. Ecology of blackbird social systems. Ecol. Monogr. 31:285-312.

Palmer, R.S., (ed) 1976. Handbook of N.A. birds vols. 2 & 3, waterfowl. Yale Univ. Press, New Haven. 600p.

Parks, G.H., and Parks, H.C., 1963. Notes on trip to Evening Grosbeak nesting. Bird-Banding 34:22-30.

Payne, R.B., 1965. Egg size & numbers of Brownheaded Cowbird. Condor 67(1):44-60.

1983. Distributional checklist of birds of Michigan. Museum of Zoology, Univ. of Michigan, Ann Arbor.

Paynter, R.A., Jr., 1954. Kent Island Tree Swallows. Bird-Banding 25(2):35-58.

Peakall, D.B., 1970. Eastern Bluebird's breeding season. Living Bird 9:239-255.

Petersen, A., and Young, H., 1950. Study of Bronzed Grackle nests. Auk 67:466-476.

Peterson, R.T., 1980. Field Guide to Birds East of Rockies. Houghton Mifflin Co., Boston. 270p.

Pickens, A.L., 1936. Nesting of Ruby-throated Hummingbirds. Wilson Bull. 48:80-85.

Pickwell, G.B., 1931. Prairie Horned Lark. Trans. Acad. of Sci. of St. Louis. Vol. 27. 153p.

Pitelka, F.A., 1942. Population of breeding birds within artificial habitat. Condor 44:172-174.

Pough, R.H., 1949. Audubon Bird Guide: Eastern Land Birds. Doubleday & Co., Inc. N.Y. 312p.

Prescott, K.W., 1965. Scarlet Tanager, New Jersey State Mus. Investigations No. 2. 159p.

Putnam, L.S., 1949. Life history of Cedar Waxwing. Wilson Bull. 61(3):141-182.

Reller, A.W., 1972. Behavioral ecology of Red-headed & Red-bellied Woodpeckers. Am. Midl. Nat. 88(2):270-290.

Root, R.B., 1967. Niche pattern of Blue-gray Gnatcatcher. Ecol. Monogr. 37:317-350.

1970. Behavior & reproductive success of Blue-gray Gnatcatcher. Condor 71(1):16-31.

Samuel, D.E., 1971. Breeding of Barn & Cliff Swallows in WV. Wilson Bull. 83(3):284-301.

Schrantz, F.G., 1943. Nest life of eastern Yellow Warbler. Auk 60(3):367-387.

Southern, W.E., 1958. Nesting of Red-eyed Vireo in Douglas Lake region, Mich. Jack-Pine Warbler 36:105-130, 185-207.

Stein, R.C., 1958. Characteristics of two populations of Alder Flycatchers. N.Y. State Mus. & Sci. Serv. Bull., 371:1-63.

Stewart, R.E., 1953. Life history of Yellowthroat. Wilson Bull. 65(2):99-115.

Stokes, A.W., 1950. Breeding behavior of Goldfinch. Wilson Bull. 62:107-127.

Summers-Smith, D., 1958. Nest-site selection, pair formation, and territory in House Sparrow. Ibis 100:120-203.

Sutton, G.M., 1927. Flocking, mating, nesting habits of prairie Horned Lark. Wilson Bull. 39(3):131-141.

Thomas, R.H., 1946. Study of Eastern Bluebirds in Ark. Wilson Bull. 58:143-183.

Vernor, J., 1965. Breeding of long-billed Marsh Wren. Condor 67:6-30.

Walkinshaw, L.H., 1938a. Life history of Eastern Goldfinch Part I. Jack-Pine Warbler 16:3-11, 14-15.

1939a. Life history of Eastern Goldfinch Part II. Jack-Pine Warbler 17:3-12.

1944. Eastern Chipping Sparrow in Mich. Wilson Bull. 56:193-205.

Weaver, R.L., 1942. Growth of English Sparrows. Wilson Bull. 56:193-205.

Weaver, R.L., and West, F.H., 1943. Breeding of the Pine Siskins. Auk 60:492-504.

Welter, W.A., 1935. Natural history of long-billed Marsh Wren. Wilson Bull. 47:3-34.

Wiens, J.A., 1969. Ecological relationship among grassland birds. Am. Ornith. Union. Ornith. Monogr. No. 8. 93p.

Williamson, P., 1971. Feeding of Red-eyed Vireo. Ecol. Monogr. 41(2): 129-152.

Williamson, P., & Gray, L. 1975. Foraging of the European Starling in Maryland. Condor 77(1):84-89.

Young, H., 1955. Breeding & nesting of Robin. Am. Midl. Nat. 53:329-252.

160